PORTRAITS OF THE
•RIVERBOATS•

PORTRAITS OF THE
•RIVERBOATS•

William C. Davis

THUNDER BAY
P·R·E·S·S

Published in the United States by
Thunder Bay Press
An imprint of the Advantage Publishers Group
5880 Oberlin Drive, San Diego, CA 92121-4794
www.advantagebooksonline.com

ISBN 1-57145-493-4
Library of Congress Cataloging-in-Publication Data available upon request.

CREDITS

Project Manager: Ray Bonds
Designers: Interprep Ltd
Picture research: Anne Lang
Production: Phillip Chamberlain
Reproduction: Media Print (UK) Limited
Printed in China

THE AUTHOR

William C. Davis has written more than thirty books on American history,
particularly of the Civil War period, including two that have achieved Pulitzer
Prize nominations. He has acted as consultant and advisor to many organizations
and frequently gives entertaining lectures during riverboat tours. He is Professor of
History and Director of Programs for the Virginia Center for Civil War Studies at
Virginia Tech.

PRELIM PHOTOGRAPHS

Page 1: The mighty sternwheel of the towboat *Sprague* churns
the water during a mid-river maneuver.
Page 2: The *Sunrise* on the cotton levee at New Orleans.
Page 3: Racing on the Ohio, 1928. On this occasion, *Chris Greene* (right) took
all the glory from Betsey Ann, but was later damaged in an horrific fire.
Page 5: The magnificent *Belle of the Bends* draws the crowds to the
Vicksburg landing on the Mississippi in about 1910.
Page 6: The *America* hard at work shifting thousands of cotton bales in about 1915
at a time when the pickings were obviously still good.

CONTENTS

INTRODUCTION

The concept of America always meant imagination, dreams of unseen vistas beyond the endless horizon, ideas to link men and the land for growth and exploitation, schemes to harness new ideas to solve old problems. For generations, from the discovery of steam power to the conquest of electricity, it was other peoples who made the raw discoveries, but Americans who tethered them to practical utility and solutions that enabled them to spread across a continent and produce an industrial and technological giant to lead nations.

Certainly that was so with harnessing steam. Steam power had actually been known to the ancients. Some 2,000 years ago priests used an ingenious system that had steam automatically opening and closing heavy temple doors. The Romans developed and used a crude form of pipe organ, and through the centuries thereafter thoughtful men occasionally invented some curiosity that used steam to move a part or make a noise. But not until James Watt did someone perfect a practical system for making steam provide power that could be transferred to some practical purpose. Soon James Stevenson would use Watt's idea to power the first locomotive, thus inaugurating the railroad era.

But it was in young America that another inventor had a different idea. John Fitch, watchmaker and failure extraordinaire, conceived the idea of running a river boat on steam, to move passengers and freight faster and cheaper than wagons and coaches. He built his *The Steamboat*, as he called it, and operated it and its successors intermittently for months in the late 1700s before his abominable business skills bankrupted him. He would be all but forgotten, and another later man, Robert Fulton, would get credit as father of the steamboat. Yet all Fulton did was take Fitch's ideas and make them more practical by being a better businessman.

It paid off for Fulton, and for the thousands who would follow him. The eastern rivers like the Hudson offered only limited scope for steamboats, however. His dream from the first was to ply the Mississippi and its tributaries, where there could be fortunes to be made by carrying settlers and cargoes from Pittsburgh to Louisville, and on to Memphis, Natchez, New Orleans, St. Louis, and more. The right boats could navigate all the way to the Minnesota territory, or west across Missouri and Nebraska to the Yellowstone, or southeast on the Tennessee to Chattanooga and Knoxville, and on the Cumberland to Nashville. The entire middle third of the continent was reachable by

Left: A Great Lakes steamer under construction at the Detroit Shipbuilding Company's yard between 1909 and 1913.

Right: Dwarfed by other riverboats during a twentieth century pageant, Norwich proudly proclaims herself to be the oldest steamboat in the world – "built 1836."

Below: The 37-foot diameter stern wheel of the Sprague, thought to be the world's largest tow boat, undergoes repairs at Baton Rouge, Louisiana.

steamboat if the bottom was good and the boat properly built. Nothing in history had ever offered such promise for opening a new world.

It would not come overnight, of course. Fulton's first western steamboat, the *New Orleans*, made an epic voyage from Pittsburgh to New Orleans in 1811-12, passing through good luck many a hazard that would claim its later counterparts. Moreover, the *New Orleans* was not powerful enough to steam back upriver against the current. But soon more boats were built, with more powerful engines, learning the lessons of the early voyages, and by 1817 a few paddlewheelers were going back up the Mississippi as far as Natchez, then Vicksburg, and eventually to Memphis. Before long, the rivers were conquered, the traffic moving freely in all directions, subject only to weather and river conditions. The heyday of the steamboats had begun.

The distant sound of a whistle, the thrashing of paddlewheels, and the appearance around the bend in the river of a large, flat-bottomed boat with high smoke stacks and either a sternpaddle or sidepaddles usually sent smaller craft scurrying. For the steamboat had right of way, and held its own on the Mississippi, Missouri, and other rivers for more than fifty years

The era of the steamboats was a fascinating part of the growth of America. They played a role in both its economic and social advance, and provided a romanticism and color that will never come again. In the early days, a journey from New orleans to St. Louis could require nearly a month. Often, the journeys presaged the development of frontier communities, for on each voyage the passengers became their own law as they steamed through lands with no other law at all. Everyone mixed irrespective of wealth or station, for space was too cramped to allow distinction of class. They also decided punishments for offenders, like thieves and pickpockets, and the will of the majority ruled. It was frontier society in microcosm.

As they developed into long, low-lying "floating palaces" that embodied every luxury then known, the steamboats were also the haunt of the gambler (although not to the extent that Hollywood has portrayed them) and others anxious to relieve fare-

Left: The sternwheeler **Mary H. Miller** *undergoing repairs in a floating drydock, Vicksburg, Mississippi.*

Above: The luxurious interiors of some riverboats were a sight to behold. Here is the galleried central parlor, with clerestory, of one of the boats operated by Norfolk & Washington Steamboat Co.

Left: Dining could be done in style aboard the Anchor Line's City of St. Louis *in 1888.*

paying passengers of their wealth. The gambling fraternity may well have caused some problems for a while, but the captains knew that, if they were monitored and controlled, their cut of the action could amount to $4,000 to $5,000 a year.

Before the arrival of the railroad, the steamboat was the most comfortable and generally relaxing means of travel anywhere in the West. If one was prepared to accept and ignore the seamier side (gamblers, prostitutes, and others) and could afford to do so, one traveled first class, and was treated to the finest food, music, wines, and other comforts, since the steamboats attracted elite members of society, and some of the finest chefs and noted musicians, many from Europe. But less well off passengers were not neglected: while they may have had to bring their own food, the banjo and piano abounded for their entertainment, and later came the steam calliope, an organ-like instrument that was much admired – even though the operator risked being scalded from burst pipes!

No one would ever be able to count the number of paddlewheelers that eventually plied the rivers. Sternwheelers, sidewheelers, centerwheelers – every configuration man could devise to meet the demands

of the river and its currents – appeared on the waters. Their engines grew from tiny short-stroke single boiler affairs, to massive creations powerful enough to drive hundreds of tons at speed against the current. They would be powerful enough to race each other upstream, and sleek enough to skim over the water, dodging the snags and sawyers and the rocky bottoms, and all the other hazards the river had to offer. They could not miss them all the time, however, and hundreds – perhaps thousands – met their ends as their hulls were ripped out by the end of a submerged tree.

They were certainly ungainly craft, not the sleek, stately riverboats of later decades. They drew only a few feet of water in their bows, while their decks sat low, barely above the water, and freight, livestock, passengers, and operating machinery often all shared much the same space. Mechanically, and compared with modern vessels, steamboats were primitive, but for their time they were remarkably efficient. The tall smoke stacks created powerful drafts and, if the boat was a wood-burner, they were designed to keep the huge sparks clear of the vessel. In fact, if the wood-burning steamboat carried cotton, as many as eight men were kept fully employed watching with water

Left: The famous **Robt. E. Lee** *shortly after her great race with the* **Natchez** *in 1870, alongside the* **Great Republic** *(later the* **Grand Republic***) at Cairo, Illinois.*

Right: The **Josie W** *leaves Tuscaloosa, pushing her "tow" toward Mobile, Alabama.*

*Above: A fine picture by the famous Civil War photographer Mathew B. Brady of the **Spaulding** arriving at the James River Landing, Virginia.*

*Above: Black roustabouts and passengers alike pose aboard the packet **City of Paducah**, Pittsburg Landing, Tenn, in 1892.*

buckets handy as the sparks streamed down like a fireworks display.

But there was also the danger of a boiler explosion. Charles Dickens made a trip on a steamboat in 1842, and was informed that "the steamboats generally blow up forward," which was apparently true, so in order to avoid contact with the boilers, the best accommodation was in the stern. Fuel used was more often coal than wood, but when racing, either against time or another vessel, kegs of resin, turpentine or even pork fat were heaved into the fireboxes.

The most terrible steamboat disaster in history was the loss of the overloaded *Sultana* in 1865, when her leaky boilers exploded and over 1,545 men, mostly returning Union veterans, perished. A high-ranking officer of the Army reported on the disaster:

"It is the common opinion among engineers that an explosion of steam boilers is impossible when they have the *proper quantity of water in them, but boilers may burst from an over-pressure of steam when they are full of water, owing to some defective part of the iron, in which there is generally no harm done than giving way of the defective part and the consequent escape of steam. One engineer who is said to be the most reliable on the river, says that even in such a case the great power of the steam, having once found a yielding place, tears everything before it, producing the effect of an explosion, and his view seems to be reasonable. What is usually understood as the explosion of the boiler is caused by the sudden development of an intense steam by the water coming in contact with red-hot iron, which produces an effect like the firing of gunpowder in a mine, and the destruction of the boilers and the boat that carries them is the consequence."*

If steamboats were the greatest revolution in transportation of their age, they were also the most dangerous. In one recorded period over some thirty-

Below: A Harper's **Weekly** *depiction of the* **Sultana,** *which exploded and sank in one of the world's worst maritime disasters.*

Above: **Seth Low,** *one of the smaller workorse sidewheelers used by the Federals during the Civil War, calls in for coals.*

Below: Wrecked and wallowing in the Ohio in April 1917, the **Tell City** *suffered the fate of many of her forebears.*

nine years during the 1800s there were 44 collisions, 166 fires, 209 boiler explosions, and no fewer than 576 sinkings from striking obstacles in the water. But the profits justified the risk, and steamboatmen were a risk-taking generation. A single boat could recoup its cost for an owner after only two or three years' operation if business was brisk. No wonder that the average life of a paddlewheeler on the big river trade was no more than six or seven years before it either went down in flames or on a snag, or else was broken up by its owner so that he could reuse its machinery and appointments in a newer, larger boat.

Soon everyone who could afford one of several classes of passage was using the boats, from paying a minimum fare for a place to stand and sleep on the deck, to hiring a luxurious state room. The main cabins offered some of the finest dining fare available anywhere, and in time there would be entertainments as well, and always a little informal gambling for those so inclined. From early days, certain rules of behavior prevailed on the boats, requiring genteel manners, respect for fellow passengers, and above all deference to the captain or master, who ruled the boat as his personal fiefdom. Indeed, though his domain was small, he was perhaps the most absolute ruler ever seen in America, for on his judgment rested the lives of his passengers and the safety of his cargo. Moreover, once the boats became "packets" and started carrying the United States mail, the responsibility grew even greater.

Fulton originally hoped to dominate steamboat trade, and even secured from Congress a patent granting him exclusive rights to operate boats on the Mississippi and its tributaries. But that could not withstand the inevitable competition, and though he would file complaints against other boat operators, his monopoly disintegrated, and Fulton himself never would become a force on the rivers. But by the time of the Civil War, large companies did begin to emerge, and after the war there would be fleets operated by the Anchor Line and Streckfus Steamers, Thomas Leathers, John Cannon, and more. Eventually their floating palaces would bring the heights of luxury and refinement to their boats, some of the vessels being

Below: **Henry Frank** *with the biggest load of cotton ever carried on the Mississippi – 9,226 bales – during the 1880s. If she had space, she would take passengers too.*

Right: Black roustabouts take a breather from hauling bales of cotton on the busy New Orleans waterfront. Theirs was vital work, but they were paid little.

Above: Provided the bill would be paid the packet **James Lee** *would carry any cargo, from* **U.S. Mail** *to wagons.*

Above: A group of fashionable passengers enjoy a Sunday afternoon cruise on the hurricane roof of the **City of St. Louis** *in 1889.*

compared to floating wedding cakes for their decorative delicacy.

Before then, the Civil War had made something quite different of steam traffic. The rivers were the key to control of the new Confederacy, and the Union would campaign to seize control of them to split the South in two with the conquest of the Mississippi, and split it again by controlling the Tennessee and Cumberland. Without the rivers the North could not have won the war as it did, and it developed distinctive paddlewheel-driven warships to do so. Ironclads, tinclads, woodclads, even cottonclads, became common sights, as both North and South used whatever material they could to armor and protect the converted packets and purpose-built warships that carried their war on the waters. The Union's domination of the rivers, thanks to more, newer, and better steam vessels, was an important part of winning the war itself.

Meanwhile, a distinctive culture grew up along the river, tied intimately to the steamboats themselves. Their arrival in port was always an occasion. Young boys dreamed of being pilots, and one such youngster, Samuel L. Clemens, actually would become a pilot for a time before he went on to become the great writer Mark Twain, who left behind such a vivid portrait of the world he had known in his *Life on the Mississippi*. In 1844 one proud steamboatman boasted that "it takes a man to ride one of these half alligator boats, head on a snag, high pressure, valve sodered [sic] down, 600 souls on board & in danger of going to the devil."

The men who worked on the boats were a special breed, worldly, adventurous, sometimes a bit rowdy. They invented their own tall tales and became cultural characters in their own right, and the places they stayed and played when ashore, like Natchez-Under-the-Hill, became storied for wickedness and violence. Yet most were simply working men with a feel for travel and freedom.

As the decades passed, more and more vessels plied the rivers, stretching even farther west until, by the 1870s, there were even steamboats on the Yellowstone, almost within sight of the continental divide. Meanwhile, on the Pacific side of the divide, steam was eventually brought around Cape Horn to San Francisco Bay, and from there the boats plied the Sacramento River and the San Joaquin, in support of a settlement that had already been built by dogged frontiersmen.

After the Civil War, it was cotton that drove the industry on the Mississippi well toward the end of the century, before railroad expansion finally took over. In the twentieth century, the paddlewheelers went into decline against competition from the railroads and the newer American love affair with the automobile. They could go anywhere, while the boats, by definition, could only follow the rivers. The great steamboat operators dwindled, the boats were broken up or converted to wharfboats and barges, and by World War II there were only a few dozen still operating, most of them either working as tow boats, or else converted into day excursion boats for dinner, dancing, or gambling, out of ports like St. Louis and New Orleans. Otherwise the remnants of this once incredible industry were mostly to be seen tied up rotting in shipyards, or beached along the river among the cottonwoods, landmarks of perhaps a more leisurely time that had come and gone.

But then came a resurgence. Anxious not to lose touch with their past, Americans discovered a new love affair with the paddlewheelers thanks to the saving and refitting of the *Delta Queen*. Ironically, she was built in Ireland, and had spent her early career operating in California on the Sacramento River. But once she was brought to the Mississippi in the 1950s and put into operation as an overnight tourist steamboat, she quickly came to symbolize for new generations what steamboating had been for their ancestors. In the next forty years more new steamboats would be built and put into service, so that now there are three overnight vessels on the Mississippi and its tributaries, another on the Columbia River in the Northwest, a fleet about to start plying the Intercoastal Waterway on the Atlantic shore, and a score and more of others making day trip excursions out of cities from St. Paul to New Orleans. America's love affair with the steamboat, it seems, has entered a new phase of infatuation, one that has spread to the rest of the world, as people come from all around the globe now to sit in a rocking chair on the Texas deck of a steamboat, sipping a cool drink, and watching the world pass by at seven miles an hour.

It is as hypnotic now as it was almost two centuries ago when Nicholas Roosevelt and his wife Lydia and their Labrador retriever Tiger made that first voyage

Above: War supplies are loaded aboard the **Robert Morris** *at the lower wharf at Yorktown, captured by Mathew Brady in 1862.*

Right: Roustabouts take a break from loading barrels by shooting craps on the lower deck of the **City of St. Louis**, *1889.*

from Pittsburgh to New Orleans. Many of the sights are still the same, for all the work of time and erosion and the efforts to control the rivers with locks and dams. The heron still skim along the banks, the fish still jump from the water, the willows still wave in the westerly breezes. In spite of the oil refineries and the gravel works, there are still places where a steamboater can inhale the scent of the wilderness. And on the quiet of a summer night on the river, with only the faint chug of the engine and the sound of the paddlewheel churning the river at a stately seventeen revolutions per minute, one can still look up into a cloudless sky and watch the stars seemingly spin as the boat turns and twists along Big Muddy or Old Man River or the Mighty Mo.

Some things never change, and as long as men still feel the romance of the river and the lure of a remarkable tradition, there will be steamboats on the water, and men and women to seek the tranquility of a journey back in time.

Far left: Loaded with day trippers, the **Hendrick Hudson** *in New York's Bear Mountain Park.*

Left: Sunday strollers pass the **America** *on the levee at New Orleans, 1906.*

Above left: Today, people can still enjoy the pleasures of glitzy paddlewheelers such as the **Belle of Louisville.**

Above: Day trippers enjoy the ride as the **White Horse** *negotiates the Five Finger Rapids, Alaska.*

THE *NEW ORLEANS* – THE FIRST

Lamentably, much is not known about the first practical steamboat to ply the western waters. Indeed, the origin of steamboating itself is the subject of much controversy, though abundant evidence establishes that the forgotten pioneer John Fitch had built and operated a working steamboat, an unnamed little vessel that carried passengers on the Delaware River, for several months in 1790. But then steamboating languished for seventeen years until Robert Fulton operated his first vessel, which he simply called *The Steamboat*, then renamed it *The North River Steamboat of Clermont*, which history eventually shortened to *Clermont*. But Fulton knew that the real money in steamboating was not on the short, shallow rivers of the Atlantic seaboard, but on the Ohio and Mississippi, and soon he went to work on what was to be his truly pioneering venture.

The *New Orleans* emerged from a builder's yard outside Pittsburgh, even as Fulton and his partners obtained the seemingly impossible from Congress – a patent granting exclusive monopoly to all steamboat operation on the great rivers. The first to exercise that right was a sidewheel vessel about 148 feet long, and perhaps 32 feet in the beam, that cost Fulton and his partners $38,000 to construct. She had a single deck with just two cabins, one for the ladies aft and well appointed with curtains on the windows and a carpet on the floor, and another cabin forward for the gentlemen, which also doubled as a communal dining room. Beyond these bare features, not much more is known of her appearance, and the reconstruction that was done many years later and shown in this photograph is highly conjectural.

What is not conjecture is the drama of her first voyage from September 1811 to the spring of 1812. Everywhere she went she caused wonder and consternation. The master Nicholas Roosevelt's wife Lydia came along, even though pregnant, and gave birth to her baby in Louisville. They steamed right through the worst of the famed New Madrid earthquakes, saw islands disappear in the natural catastrophe, were chased by Indians, and were nearly wrecked a host of times, and yet finally made it to New Orleans and the record books. The life of the *New Orleans* was brief after that, however. With her engines too weak to power her back upstream any distance, she plied back and forth between New Orleans and Natchez until she struck a snag and sank a year later.

CINCINNATI WATERFRONT IN 1848

Steamboats captured the imagination of America's artists just as much as they did that of young Americans themselves, and nowhere was this more true than with photographers. The art of making images on copper and silver, then glass and paper, was introduced just as the paddlewheelers were taking over the western rivers in the 1840s, and as soon as cameramen developed the ability to take their instruments outdoors to make landscape images, the steamboats became among their earliest subjects.

Probably the finest and most famous of all early steamboat images were made by the Cincinnati firm of Fontayne & Porter. In the fall of 1848 they took their daguerreotype camera – an instrument that made images on sensitized polished copper plates covered with silver – across the Ohio River to the Kentucky shore, and then set about making a panorama of the Cincinnati waterfront compiled from eight separate images. The clarity produced by the lengthy exposures required was breathtaking, the more so for the details it shows of early steamboats built before the vogue for gingerbread decoration and frills took hold.

At center sits the *Embassy*, a side-wheeler fresh off the ways at the Wheeling shipyard where she was built. Just a few months later she would see her boilers collapse, killing ten men aboard and injuring twenty-five others. Next to her is tied up the *Car of Commerce*, newly built at Murraysville, Virginia, on the Ohio, and destined for disaster within a few months in December when she tore out her bottom on the falls of the Ohio at Louisville and sank downstream. Both vessels have only two full decks above the waterline, while the *Embassy* shows a vestige of a third one that would soon become standard and full length on almost all packets. It had already become customary for boats to place the names of the several states on their cabin doors, thus making cabins into "state rooms," and after the admission of Texas in 1845, when a third deck began to be added to accommodate boat's officers, steamboaters came to call it the Texas deck. The Texas on the *Embassy* shows the new deck in embryo. Within twenty years every passenger packet on the big rivers would have three and even four decks, and this already teeming waterfront would be crowded with a forest of smokestacks and gleaming white monarchs of the rivers.

NATCHEZ-UNDER-THE-HILL

Of all of the storied places associated with the steamboat era on the Mississippi, none attracted more legend, or a more unsavory reputation, than a few square blocks of warehouses, gambling dens, saloons, and brothels on a low lying plateau beneath the Mississippi bluff topped by Natchez. Called "Under-the-Hill" thanks to its location, and today largely gone thanks to floods and erosion, it once conjured images of debauchery, crime, and sinister deeds by night.

In fact, it began as the landing for Natchez, which it remains to this day, and such places were not uncommon with bluff cities like Memphis, Columbus, and others. Natchez-Under-the-Hill had already become a notorious place even before the steamboat era, however, mainly due to its being a major landing for the keelboatmen and flatboatmen who earlier brought produce downriver. Many of them completed their voyages in Natchez, got their wages, and spent it in the saloons and bordellos, and then walked back to Kentucky on the fabled Natchez Trace that started just outside town. When the steamboats came, Natchez was already one of the wealthiest communities in America, and where there was money and commerce, there was bound to be an industry catering to those who worked hard and wanted to blow off steam.

Under-the-Hill never really lived up to its reputation, but when the steamboats landed and the crews wanted a good time, they usually went no farther than the dens and pits near the landing. Few fortunes were lost there, but many a deck hand was skinned of his wages. For all the stories of duels and murders, they were few, though dangerous men like James Bowie were to be seen there, and the famous Sandbar Fight – really a brawl rather than a duel – took place just a mile or so up the bank. Mainly, Under-the-Hill was a working district just like those in many another American river town, where the business was just business, even if sometimes a bit seedy. To the weary boatmen, it meant a few hours or days of fun before the next voyage. Even today, when the few overnight steamboats still on the Mississippi tie up at Natchez, the crew anxiously await permission to get ashore and "go under the hill" for a night of fun off the boat, though today the gambling is done on a licensed gambling "boat" permanently tied up on the bank, and incapable of plying the river even it if wished.

BUILDING A STEAMBOAT

As with all new industries, the explosion of the paddlewheelers brought with it a number of other new technologies, or gave a quantum leap to existing trades. The first *New Orleans* was built at Pittsburgh, and thereafter the Pennsylvania city would be one of the major construction sites for the thousands of steamboats to come. Very soon, however, boatyards cropped up in a score of other places along the Ohio, and later the Mississippi. Cincinnati, Ohio, became an important boat building city, as did Jeffersonville, Indiana, and later St. Louis, Missouri. In the early days most of the construction was confined to northern cities, for in this, as in other areas, the South did not industrialize at nearly the same pace. Still, in time boatyards were to be found at Point Pleasant and Wheeling, Virginia (later West Virginia), Louisville and Paducah, Kentucky, Nashville and Johnsonville, Tennessee, and eventually New Orleans. Nevertheless, Pennsylvania, Ohio, and Indiana, would dominate steamboat building from first to last, not least because they had the facilities to make not only the boats, but also the vital steam boilers and engines.

Until late in the nineteenth century, it was an industry built of wood. That alone helped to account for the fact that so many paddlewheelers met their ends in flame. The combination of open flames from wood and coal fired boilers, boiler explosions, and wooden superstructures, almost guaranteed that any accident could lead to fire, and that any fire could be catastrophic.

A small army of carpenters and craftsmen made their living for well over a century building the boats. The fact that they were more like houses and hotels than traditional sailing vessels meant that they were built largely by the same techniques, allowing only for the necessary structural adaptations to ensure that water ran off the decks rather than into the boat.

As the boats became larger and the competition more acute, the builders made them more decorative, some being virtual gingerbread palaces. Yet it was practically all hand work done by skilled builders and millwrights until late in the 1800s, when machinery and steel began to appear on the rivers. When the steamboat era declined, towns like Jeffersonville and New Albany that had been heavily dependent on the boatyards for employment without another major industry went into a decline at the same time, and some never recovered.

THE LEVEE AT KEOKUK

Nothing quite matched the bustle to be found anywhere on the rivers that the boats tied up. When a paddlewheeler was in town, it was as if the circus had come. Children ran to the river front, ladies walked down to gaze discreetly at the passengers coming and going, and the men went aboard to look at the engines, talk to friends who worked the boats, and hear the latest political gossip and racy stories as they made their way from mouth to mouth, boat to boat, town to town, along the stream.

Keokuk, Iowa, was no exception. Here four vessels tie up at or beside the Keokuk wharf sometime around 1852 or 1853, in one of the earliest photographs of paddlewheelers taken in Iowa. The levee teems with activity. A stack of chairs at left suggests new furnishings for one of the boats' main cabins, while crates of goods stretch on down to the water line. There are sacks of grain and bales of goods, and teamsters with wagons and teams ready to haul them to the merchants in town.

The boats themselves are representative of the unglamorous but hardy backbone of river commerce. At left sits the *Kate Swinney*, a sidewheeler built in 1852 to carry tobacco, but which later traveled the upper Missouri on the fur trade. She went to the bottom in 1855, and her poor crew, having escaped the sinking, were caught and killed by Native Americans. Next to her sits the *Federal Arch*, built in 1850, and operating as a packet out of St. Louis and Louisville until 1856, when she was caught in ice at St. Louis and crushed. Next to her sits the *Belle Gould*, built in 1852 at New Albany, Indiana, to run between St. Louis and Keokuk. She also ran on the Illinois River up to Peoria before she hit a snag on the Mississippi below Cairo and went to the bottom in 1854. And at far right sits the *U. S. Mail*, also built in 1852, at Pittsburgh. She, too, was a hard luck boat, being rammed and sunk within a year of launch, then raised and put on the Missouri River operating out of St. Louis, only to hit a snag and go to the bottom in Kansas in 1857.

Once the Mississippi was again in Union hands, the commerce interrupted by more than two years of war could resume once more. It was a commerce that was vital to the whole continent, for more than half of America's navigable rivers drained into the Mississippi, making New Orleans the most important and thriving port in the country. Grain from Minnesota and Nebraska, coal from West Virginia, iron and steel from Pittsburgh, tobacco and hemp from Kentucky, and livestock from two dozen states, all had to come down the Mississippi to find markets or to be shipped to the East or abroad. The war and Confederate control of the river at Vicksburg and elsewhere had put an end to most of that trade, but once it opened again everyone scrambled to get their goods moving.

Never before the Civil War was there such an explosion of steamboat building. The yards at St. Louis and Mound City and Cincinnati and Jeffersonville and New Albany and Pittsburgh and more, teemed with workmen producing new vessels to carry the burgeoning trade, and for most of them the greatest prize was to put into the New Orleans wharf. Virtually hundreds of vessels were operating on the Mississippi by 1864, bringing with them renewal of all of the ancillary trades upon which steamboats depended. Mechanics and steam fitters were employed again. Wood lots along the banks provided income for farmers and wood cutters providing fuel. Hotels and restaurants saw travelers and businessmen return, and the dreams of a generation of young boys like Sam Clemens (Mark Twain) gained renewal in the hope that maybe they, too could become steamboat captains.

Here the wharf at the foot of Canal Street in the Crescent City teems with a line of steamboats that reaches to the horizon, most of them double-stackers and one with the trademark "Indian feathers" sticking up from the top of its stacks. Bales of cotton lie in the foreground awaiting shipment, while a line of carriages – the taxis of their day – stand awaiting the business of carrying passengers to the city's hostelries and counting houses. New Orleans did not suffer much during the war, for she was a Confederate city and closed to commerce for barely a year before she fell to the Yankees again in April 1862 without a fight. For the rest of the war she would be a Union port, once more on her way to resuming her dominance as the most important port city in the reunited nation.

THE SHOWBOAT

Every bit as much a part of the river scene as the packets and the working paddlewheelers, the showboats were not in the main true steamboats. The majority, in fact, had no engines or paddlewheels, but were instead pushed or towed from port to port by other vessels, then tied up for the term of a show's run before being moved on to the next landing. The showboats grew out of a much earlier practice that began in the 1810s, when theater troups had their own boats and traveled the Mississippi and Ohio, but gave their performances ashore in theaters hired for the run. It was only a short leap of logic from that to turning their boats themselves into theaters, reducing costs, and freeing them of contractual obligations to shore houses if a run was going too well or not well enough.

The first showboat made its appearance in 1834, called a "floating theater" by its owners. It was nothing but a large room built atop a barge, loaded with actors, costumes and props, and then floated down the river. The impresario blew a trumpet whenever he tied up at a port to announce the showboat had come, played his show as long as the people came and paid, and then moved on. When he finally hit New Orleans, he gave his last shows and sold the boat for wood, then went back to Ohio to build another one and start the process anew. Thus was born the showboat.

The impresarios presented far more than plays ranging from the works of Shakespeare to the broadest of farces. They also presented sleight of hand artists, ventriloquists, animal acts, and even indefinable things called "Thaumaturgic Experiments." But it was always the acting that drew the majority of patrons down to the wharves to step aboard the sometimes gaudy, often spartan showboats. In the early days there were even "double features," two plays performed with an intermission in between, and all for an admission of one dollar. Before long audiences had the opportunity to see some of the greatest actors of the day, men like Junius Brutus Booth and Edwin Forrest.

It did not come without risk, for often the audiences were so rustic and some simply did not understand that it was all make believe. Rude hunters in the seats were known to stand and shout back at villains, or even to draw their weapons on them. It was not uncommon during the presentation of a typical bathetic story of an impoverished mother and child being turned out of their home by an evil landlord, for men in the audience to take up a collection to pay her rent. The rougher elements also gathered at the showboat, where there was drink and often a card game.

This handsome side-wheeler represented the realization of a boy's dreams. The *Aleck Scott* was built at Louisville and St. Louis in 1848, and was a big packet boat at 296 feet and 44 foot across the beam, with tonnage of 1,193. Her six boilers and 25-inch cylinders drove her comfortably at 4 knots or more on the St. Louis to New Orleans run for thirteen years before the outbreak of the Civil War. Then she was taken into service as a troop transport, and appears in this photograph taken at Cairo, Illinois, loaded with soldiers, quite possibly on the eve of her departure with the rest of the transport fleet that carried U. S. Grant's army up the Tennessee and Cumberland Rivers to attack and capture Forts Henry and Donelson in February 1862.

On May 18, 1862, the government purchased *Aleck Scott* and renamed her *Fort Henry* briefly in honor of her part in the victory. But then she became a part of the government's second wave of gunboat conversions when she was sent to St. Louis to be turned into a sister ship for the *Choctaw*, and renamed yet again, this time *Lafayette*. Unlike *Choctaw*, which had two ironclad casemates forward of her paddleboxes, the *Lafayette* was given one long casemate stretching from the paddlewheels almost all the way to her bow, which was itself fitted as a ram. The casemate sides sloped upward at an angle, and were then rounded to the top, while at the front the casemate was rounded almost hemispherically. She carried the same India rubber backing for an inch of iron plating, while her pilot house would stick up almost obtrusively, itself well armored. As with *Choctaw*, however, the idea of the rubber bouncing enemy shot off was soon proved a failure, for the rubber was more prone to rot.

Commissioned February 21, 1863, the revamped *Aleck Scott* steamed past the Vicksburg batteries, took part in the shelling of Grand Gulf, participated in the Red River Campaign the following year, and spent the rest of the war patrolling the lower Mississippi. She was eventually laid up at new Orleans and sold in March 1866.

She had been, as *Lafayette*, one of the most imposing ironclads of the war, but her greater claim to fame was as the *Aleck Scott* in the days immediately before the war. For it was then that her pilot was a man named Horace Bixby, who took under his wing and trained aboard the *Aleck Scott* a young would-be steamboat captain, Samuel L. Clemens, destined one day to be Mark Twain.

MARK TWAIN

In his classic *Life on the Mississippi*, Samuel L. Clemens, writing under his immortal pseudonym Mark Twain, declared that the steamboat captain was the most unfettered potentate on the face of the earth, a virtual king aboard his boat, with the whole world laid out before him in the panorama viewed from his pilot house. If Twain was being somewhat hyperbolic, still he spoke for how he and a generation of young American men felt about steamboating. It represented travel, independence, challenge against men and the elements, and a spirit of adventure in step with the country and the times. No wonder it attracted this most romantic of men.

Born near Florida, Missouri, November 30, 1835, young Clemens grew to adolescence in Hannibal on the Mississippi, a small town that thanks to steamboat trade soon grew to become the second largest in the state within a few years. He stayed in school until he was fourteen, then went to Washington, Philadelphia, even New York, to seek a trade, but by the time he was nineteen he was back in Missouri and infatuated with becoming a river pilot. He apprenticed himself to Horace Bixby in 1857, and worked at it until the outbreak of war four years later. He set himself the task that faced all pilots, as he said, "the stupendous task of learning the twelve hundred miles of the Mississippi River between St. Louis and New Orleans – of knowing it as exactly and unfailingly, even in the dark, as one knows the way to his own features." For the rest of his life, the characters he met on the river would return to populate his books and sketches, while he would himself ever after romanticize his days at the pilot wheel. Yet he also saw firsthand the darker side of a steamboater's life, for his brother Hendry was working on the Pennsylvania when an explosion in 1858 mortally injured him in scalding steam. Sam Clemens sat at his brother's side to watch the tortured young man die.

In later years Twain spoke of dreaming of returning to the river life, yet as an old man he actually had nightmares about being forced back aboard steamboats. Late in life he made a nostalgic steamboat trip from St. Paul to New Orleans to retrace the route of his young adventures that formed so much of the matrix of his literary success. Life may have taken him from the river, but it could never take the river from Mark Twain, and with his pen and imagination he gave it to the world.

America's early wars scarcely used the rivers. During the Revolution there was no steamboat, and even during the so-called War of 1812, the practical steamboat came to the Mississippi and Ohio only in the months before the war commenced, and played no role in it subsequently. When war with Mexico erupted in 1846, for the first time soldiers and steamboats came together, since the bulk of the American Army under General Winfield Scott that marched from Vera Cruz to Mexico City first embarked aboard steamers and sailboats out of New Orleans. Those volunteers, in turn, often came to New Orleans itself on paddlewheelers from Pittsburgh, Louisville, Memphis, and Vicksburg. For the majority of those boys, it was a triple adventure: their first trip away from home, their first voyage on a steamboat, and their first experience of war.

Americans were not a great deal more sophisticated some years later in 1861 when war broke out between North and South. Soldiers in the eastern theater of the conflict, between the Atlantic seaboard and the Alleghenies, rarely if ever set foot on a riverboat except for a few amphibious operations along the coast. Out west of the mountains, however, the rivers would be the highways for hundreds of thousands of officers and men going to war. The Union Army would eventually operate fleets of its own transports, like the USS *Brown* shown here tied up off Cairo, Illinois, a major Northern staging area as well as site of one of its principal navy yards. When an army corps on the move, like William T. Sherman's headed for Vicksburg at the end of 1862, could number 30,000 or more, it would require dozens of such transports to get the men to their assignment. Moreover, throughout U. S. Grant's campaign to take control of the Mississippi with his army, even when marching overland he always had to have transports nearby to handle maneuvers such as his bypassing of Vicksburg to land his army below the city and move against it from the rear.

When not carrying troops to action, the *Brown* and its innumerable sisters ferried supplies, and carried the wounded upriver to the great hospitals at Memphis, Nashville, Cairo, and other cities. Most of them had been prewar commercial vessels, purchased or commandeered into service, and giving a vital performance in the struggle to conquer the rivers and use them to preserve the Union.

LOST TO A "TORPEDO" – THE USS *CAIRO*

The great workhorses of the Union's western river fleet were the "city class" ironclad steamboats designed by the brilliant engineer James B. Eads, and constructed by naval builder Samuel Pook at shipyards in St. Louis, Missouri, and Mound City and Cairo, Illinois. They grew out of Eads's interest in converting the salvage boat *Benton* into a warship, and when that was first vetoed, he set about designing his own specially adapted vessels to cruise the often shallow waters of the Mississippi and its tributaries. The result was a wholly new kind of river craft, to be known by a number of names – Eads gunboats, Pook "turtles" after their builder and their appearance, "city class" boats since most were named for river towns, and officially as the Cairo class.

Eads would build seven of them, starting with the *St. Louis*, which he finished in just forty-five days. They were 175 feet in length, with a 75-foot beam, and drew just 6 feet of water. Each carried thirteen large cannon inside a slanting casemate covered with two feet of solid oak for protection, with more than two inches of railroad iron protecting the bow and the amidships where the engines stood. Eads mounted the paddlewheel at the stern within the casemate. Ironically, Eads built them for the United States Army and not the Navy, and virtually all of their service would be under overall Army command.

The *St. Louis, Cairo, Carondelet, Mound City, Cincinnati, Louisville*, and *Pittsburgh* carried most of the burden of the river war right to the end. The *Cairo* became perhaps the best known, not for its exploits in action, but for its spectacular death. Patrolling the Yazoo River near Vicksburg, Mississippi, on December 12, 1862, to remove underwater mines, she simultaneously struck two of them herself and went to the bottom in just twelve minutes, her back broken. Incredibly, there was no loss of life or serious injury, and when the sailors reached shore or the other boats of the squadron, all they could see remaining of *Cairo* were the tops of her stacks peeking above the surface. She had made history in a tragic way, being the first major warship to go to the bottom at the hands of an underwater mine, or "torpedo" as they were then called. There she remained for the next century, until her hulk was raised for preservation and display at the Vicksburg National Battlefield Park, where visitors today can walk aboard an actual Civil War gunboat.

THE USS *BENTON* – MATCHLESS FIREPOWER

Ironically, the steam warship that saw the greatest service during the Civil War was never supposed to be a gunboat at all. She began life as a centerwheel catamaran snag boat, built on two hulls twenty feet apart, which allowed her to position herself directly over a submerged tree snag or other navigational hazard, in order to pull it out of the bottom mud to clear the channel. She was named for Senator Thomas Hart Benton of Missouri. Just over 200 feet long and 72 feet in the beam, she drew 9 feet of water, and immediately attracted the attention of engineer James B. Eads at the outset of the war. Snag boats had very powerful engines to enable them to wrest obstructions, and Eads realized that such an engine could handle the massive weight of armor plating and heavy guns.

At first the Navy turned down Eads's suggestion of converting the *Benton* into a warship at the outbreak of war, and Eads went on to design his Cairo class gunboats. But he did not give up on the *Benton*, and soon started her conversion, joining the two hulls to make them stronger, and then built the most imposing casemate to be seen on the river, three and one-half inches of railroad iron plating every surface except the stern. Inside he placed sixteen big guns – two 9-inch smoothbores, seven 32-pounder smoothbores, and seven 42-pounder rifles – in a battery of four in the bow, five on each side, and two at the stern. Though all that weight slowed her to just five knots, nothing on the rivers could match *Benton* for firepower.

Commissioned February 24, 1862, she saw constant service thereafter, first as flagship of the Mississippi Squadron. She fought at Island Number 10, Fort Pillow, Memphis, ran the batteries at Vicksburg and participated in the bombardment of the city, in the 1864 Red River expedition, and captured the Confederate ironclad *Missouri* at the end of the war. She suffered her own tragedy in the Yazoo River, just as did Eads's *Cairo*. Two weeks after *Cairo* went to the bottom, *Benton*'s captain Lieutenant Commander W. Gwin was killed during skirmishing with Confederates ashore, making him one of the very few ships' captains to lose his life during the war. At the end of the conflict, like so many other gallant vessels that had done their part and more, there was no peacetime use for such a lumbering, muscle-bound ship in the seagoing Navy, and she was decommissioned on July 20, 1865, at Mound City, and sold four months later at auction to end her days in the scrap yard.

THE "WOODCLAD" *LEXINGTON*

The North was not at all prepared to fight a war on its rivers when the Civil War erupted in April 1861. Moreover, it would take months to design and build modern steam gunboats to wrestle for command of the Mississippi and its tributaries in Confederate territory. Until that could be done, Washington realized it must depend on ersatz improvisations with what was already at hand. Hundreds of river steamboats were already in the water, but many would require too much time and expense in conversion, while none had any sort of armor or protection against the powerful cannon that the Confederates placed in river batteries on bluffs at a dozen places on the Mississippi.

The most immediate solution was to purchase a few existing steamboats that seemed suitable, and the task was given to Commander John Rodgers of the United States Navy. In June 1861 he bought three wooden sidewheelers, the *Lexington*, the *Conestoga*, and the *A. G. Tyler*, for a total of $62,000, and then contracted with a shipbuilder to pay another $41,000 to convert them into gunboats. The *Lexington* was brand new, just launched a few weeks before at Belle Vernon, Pennsylvania. She stood 180 feet long in the water, 36 in the beam, and drew just over 6 feet. She could only make 7 knots, making her slower than many steamers, but her engine and boilers were new and well built. Rodgers had all superfluous exposed decking and cabins taken down, and ordered the boilers and most of the engine accouterments lowered below the waterline for safety, and then had five inches of solid oak added all around the exposed superstructure to protect her crew from rifle fire from shore. He also enclosed the sidewheels in paddle boxes, and reinforced the decks to carry the strain of the four 8-inch Dahlgren smoothbores and two 32-pounders mounted in broadsides behind the oak bulwarks. Because of the oak, the *Lexington*, as well as the similarly converted and armed *Conestoga* and *Tyler*, soon became known as "woodclads."

Lexington saw more service on the rivers than almost any other steam warship, starting in August 1861 with her first seizure of a Rebel steamboat, and ending with her decommissioning and sale in July 1865. Perhaps her most dangerous moment came on the Red River when she led the way for the fleet trapped above Alexandria, Louisiana, by low water. The Army built a dam to temporarily raise the water level, and when they broke the dam, Lexington was the first to ride the flood to safety.

USS *CHOCTAW* – CONVERTED FOR WAR

No sooner did the Union get converted vessels like the woodclads and the *Benton* on the water, and the city class gunboats in operation, than it began to seek even more boats for conversion into new and bigger revolutionary designs. The sidewheeler *Choctaw* had been constructed in 1855 at a massive 245 feet along the waterline, with a 38-foot beam, yet still only drawing 7 feet of water. She made a number of trips from St. Louis to New Orleans before the war, and then in 1862 her owner sold her to the Army for conversion.

She would become the most imposing of all of the second wave of gunboat conversions. Her length was extended to 280 feet, but then everything above the waterline was removed except the side wheels and some of her machinery. Instead of building one long casemate as with the previous vessels, the constructors erected a smaller one forward toward the bow, its four sides slanting toward the deck in all directions, and covered with several inches of iron plating. Inside were mounted three 9-inch smoothbores and a massive 100-pounder rifle. Amidships, just forward of the paddlewheels, they placed another casemate with two 24-pounders, while astern of the wheels two 30-pounder rifles in a third wooden casemate protected the stern. Both casemates had just an inch of iron plating, mounted over an inch of India rubber, the idea (a novel one that failed to work) being that the rubber would cushion impacts and make enemy shot bounce off the side, thus reducing the need for more heavy armor on a vessel that was already so weighted down that she could make only a few knots. The wheels themselves were covered in a protective box connected to the midship casemate, and contained as well the protected pilot house.

Choctaw went into service March 23, 1863, under Lieutenant Commander F. M. Ramsay, even though she was not yet finished and actually still had workmen aboard her. She spent the rest of the war on the Mississippi and other western rivers. With virtually all Confederate warships on the Mississippi either sunk or captured by this time, *Choctaw*'s service was primarily in cooperating with the land forces in attacking shore batteries and fortifications. She suffered fifty-three hits from Confederate batteries in operations on the Yazoo in late April 1863, and then helped take the Rebel fortifications at Haynes' Bluff, and destroyed the Confederate shipyard at Yazoo City along with several vessels under construction. In the spring of 1864 she participated in the Red River operations culminating in capture of Fort DeRussey below Alexandria, and finished her career outside New Orleans in July 1865 where she was decommissioned, and was sold eight months later.

A "Tinclad"

In the explosion of innovation in steam warships brought about by the outbreak of the Civil War, the Union government seemed to feel that there would be safety in numbers, not only numbers of ships, but of varieties of programs for putting them in the water. Even after commissioning the city class gunboats and getting the woodclads and the *Benton* under way, Washington decided to experiment with even more wooden vessels, the idea this time being to take smaller packet boats, with their speed and maneuverability, and convert them into lightly armed warships carrying only light armor as well, in order not to compromise their speed. These boats would not be pitted against the heavy guns of Confederate forts or the Rebels' own ironclads, but instead used for communications and to support land troops in action against enemy soldiers in the field where there was little danger of the boats coming against heavy artillery. They would use thin iron to protect just the pilot house and the engines and boilers against small arms fire, while covering the rest of the bulwarks with several inches of oak to shield the three or four pieces of light artillery emplaced on the decks. Somewhat derisively, these lightly armored boats were to be dubbed "tinclads."

In the end, scores of them were converted from smaller river packets, and as a result every one was different to some degree. Most were sternwheelers with very shallow draft. Some drew less than two feet of water, and were just 150 feet long and no more than 30 feet in the beam. All would have wooden bulwarks or casemates to protect the exposed decks and the men working the boat and its guns. On many, the constructors placed an inch of iron over the oak as added protection, then armed them with 12-pounders or 24-pounders, with occasionally a gun of heavier caliber if the deck could stand the strain. Most retained their prewar names, but a number went off to war with nothing more than numbers painted on their pilot houses or stacks. In the end more than sixty of them saw service on every tributary of the Mississippi, never at the forefront of battle, but always there in support of land forces, protecting communications and merchant shipping from raids by Confederates, and frequently seeing action against the likes of Nathan Bedford Forrest and other Rebel cavalrymen. One giant tinclad, the *Blackhawk*, actually became flagship for Admiral David Dixon Porter, one of the dominant commanders of the Yankee fleets on the rivers.

THE FLEET AT ANCHOR

A common sight on the Mississippi River by 1862 was a fleet like this one photographed at anchor off Mound City, Illinois. In the center of the line floats the Eads city class ironclad *St. Louis*, which launched October 12, 1861, while fore and aft of her a number of tinclads and transports sit calmly on the Ohio. In the distance, with the large paddlebox that protects her sidewheels just visible above *St. Louis'* stern, sits the timberclad *Tyler*.

In an interesting anomaly among the city class boats, *St. Louis* would have her name changed on September 8, 1862, to *Baron De Kalb*, in honor of a Bavarian soldier of fortune who came to the colonies with the Marquis de Lafayette and became himself a major general of Continental forces during the Revolution, and was mortally wounded in action in 1780. Just why Washington decided to change *St. Louis'* name is uncertain, but the result was that the *Baron De Kalb* became a "city" class ironclad that was not named for a city.

That was only the beginning of her misfortunes. As *St. Louis* she joined the Western Gunboat Fleet and participated in the successful bombardment of Fort Henry, Tennessee, in February 1862, but was then badly mauled in the attack on Fort Henry a few days later, during which she served as flagship. After that she saw service in attacks on Confederate forts at Fort Pillow and Memphis before changing names, and then went on to be transferred from the Army to the Navy and served in the Yazoo operations that saw her sister ship *Cairo* sunk by a mine. She went on to fight on Arkansas rivers, back in the Yazoo, at Haynes' Bluff, and in preliminary actions during the final Vicksburg Campaign.

But on July 13, 1863, on the Yazoo River not many miles from where the *Cairo* went down, the *Baron De Kalb* herself struck a mine, was mortally wounded like her namesake, and went to the bottom. As for the other warship in the fleet shown here, the *Tyler* served throughout the war and then suffered the ignominy of being sold for a mere $6,000 right here at Mound City, to be broken up for parts and scrap.

THE CSS STERLING PRICE

The Confederates used steamboats as well, of course, virtually their entire fleet of river warships being paddlewheelers except for the few propeller ironclads that they managed to build. But, like the Union's tin and timberclads, most were converted prewar freight and passenger boats, for the Southerners simply did not have the facilities or wherewithal to build vessels of their own from the keel up. And their small fleets of paddlewheelers were lightly armored if at all, some protected by nothing more than bales of cotton piled along the sides, leading to their being dubbed "cottonclads."

One such that enjoyed a colorful career was the CSS *General Sterling Price*. She began life in Cincinnati in 1856 as a sidewheel towboat called the *Laurent Millaudon*, sent south to work out of New Orleans for the amusingly named Good Intent Towboat Company. She was there when Louisiana seceded and the war broke out, and in January 1862 was taken over by Confederate authorities for conversion into a cottonclad. Around her sides they erected two pine bulwarks, one inside the other, and in the gap between them placed compressed cotton. They covered her sidewheels with a paddle box, mounted a pilot house atop the wheels, and then fitted a ram of four feet of oak sheathed in an inch of iron, on her bow beneath the water line. In a tactic dating back thousands of years, the Confederates hoped to make up for lack of firepower by making the entire vessel itself a weapon, driving its ram into an enemy ship beneath the waterline and thus sinking her.

To honor a current Confederate hero – soon to fall from grace – they renamed the boat the *General Sterling Price* and attached her to the River Defense Fleet. By March 25, 1862, she left for duty, even though still unfinished, and went into action in the defense of Fort Pillow on May 10. The pitifully outclassed River Defense Fleet attacked Union ironclads and actually scored some success, *Price* herself ramming and immobilizing the USS *Cincinnati* while suffering severe damage herself. But on June 6, in the naval battle between the fleets off Memphis, *Price* was herself repeatedly rammed by Yankee vessels and sank on a sandbar. In a final irony, the Federals later raised her and put her into their own service as the gunboat *General Price*, not the only case of a Union boat carrying the name of a Confederate general in this most unusual of wars.

SECRETS ABOARD THE
RIVER QUEEN

Many steamboats made history during the American Civil War, but few saw as much of it as one that was never a warship at all. The small sidewheeler *River Queen* was typical of the more modest vessels that plied the rivers and harbors of the eastern seaboard, mainly carrying passengers on day trips up the Potomac or on the Chesapeake. She had only two decks, and was no more than 150 feet in length, taken up almost entirely with passenger cabins and some room for freight below decks. She was a new boat, too, built in 1864 at Keyport, New Jersey, and sailing out of Providence, Rhode Island, briefly until she was pressed into a very special service, to become General U. S. Grant's headquarters boat at City Point on the James River as he pursued his campaign against Petersburg and Richmond, Virginia, in late 1864-65.

Just being witness to Grant and his generals in some of their high level deliberations would have been distinction enough for any vessel, especially one as otherwise unassuming as the *River Queen*. But there was much more to come. In February 1865 President Abraham Lincoln agreed to meet with a representative of the Confederate government for a discussion that might lead to a cease fire or even peace. Lincoln came to Hampton Roads, off Fort Monroe, Virginia, and Grant gave him the *River Queen* for his use in the meeting. It was there in the main cabin that Lincoln met with his old friend Alexander H. Stephens, at that time vice president of the Confederate States, and it was aboard this ship that each realized that the war would have to go on. Lincoln was willing to discuss only the reunion of North and South as a precondition to all other settlements, while Stephens was authorized to treat only on the basis of Confederate independence.

Two months later, when Richmond fell to Grant on April 2, it was the *River Queen* that brought Lincoln to Virginia once more, as he steamed up the James on April 4 to personally tour the fallen enemy capital. The sidewheeler took him back to Washington a few days later, and Lincoln was aboard her when he got the news that Robert E. Lee's army had surrendered on April 9, beginning the end of the war. That was a lot of history in which one otherwise unexceptionable little steamboat was to be both witness and participant.

THE HOSPITAL BOAT

Thanks to being largely in enemy territory, the United States river forces had to take what would normally be land-based facilities with them aboard ship wherever possible, and that was especially the case with providing care for the sick and wounded. When the shores on either side of the Mississippi were not disposed to provide succor for ailing men, the Army and Navy had to provide hospital boats to care for them instead. No one began the war prepared for the demands that it would place on the authorities to provide medical care, and the services were playing a game of catch up for quite some time as they struggled to cope, especially with the diseases and fevers endemic to the rivers of the South, and to which most Yankees had never been exposed.

As with the prewar steamboats converted to improvised action as warships and gunboats, the vessels put into service to care for the sick and wounded were not originally designed for such use. Indeed, neither government would ever design purpose-built hospital ships. Instead, they acquired existing steamboats and converted them, as with the packet boat *Nashville*, shown here tied up probably along the bank near Natchez, Mississippi, and (inset) the *Red Rover*. *Nashville* began her life as a two-decked, wooden-hulled sidewheeler built at New Albany, Indiana, in 1849, and measured 250 feet in length and 40 in the beam, displacing almost 500 tons. That made her one of the larger steamboats plying the Mississippi and Cumberland Rivers between Nashville and New Orleans.

When the war came the Washington government took her over and began the work of converting her into a hospital ship. As her photograph shows, they removed her engines and side wheels, took out her stacks and almost all other vestiges of being a steamboat, added a third deck, and made her into a hospital capable of holding 1,000 patients, though now she had to be towed wherever she went. It was an ignominious end for a once proud queen of the rivers, but her loss was the gain of the thousands of Union soldiers and sailors who could find immediate medical care and bed rest on the spot rather than having to suffer the long and often grueling trip upriver or overland to get medical attention. But when the war was over, the destiny of all powerless boats like the *Nashville* was to be sold or broken up, since the expense of reconverting them would have been too great.

Not a few steamboats during the Civil War saw service in both Union and Confederate navies, but perhaps none endured as tortured a career as the *Indianola*. She was under construction as a civilian steamer at Cincinnati in 1862, destined to be a sidewheeler of 175 feet length with an unusually wide beam of 52 feet and equally unusually powerful engines, with five boilers. In addition, two propellers were being fitted to her stern for added speed and power. But before she could be completed, a Confederate invasion of Kentucky in the fall of 1862 raised the possibility that Rebel forces might reach the Ohio and actually cross to take Cincinnati. Not wanting this powerful new vessel to fall into enemy hands, the Union commander there seized her and launched her still uncompleted on September 4, feverishly pressing work to get her turned into a warship to help defend Cincinnati if necessary. She was commissioned on September 27 and, although she was still far from completion, put in service on October 23 armed with four Dahlgren smoothbore cannon, two each fore and aft.

The Confederate threat to Cincinnati never materialized, but the *Indianola* stayed in service, trapped above Louisville by low water for a time, until she finally joined the Mississippi Squadron in January 1863. Her service would be dramatically brief, just three weeks, before she was ordered to go down the Mississippi, run past the batteries at Vicksburg, and aid in cutting off the Red River from raiding Confederates east of the Mississippi. On the night of February 13 *Indianola* steamed south and successfully passed the batteries, anchoring near Warrenton, Mississippi, then continued on her way to blockade the mouth of the Red. On February 21 she started back toward Vicksburg, but three days later was overtaken by two Confederate vessels, both recently captured from the Yankees and now turned against them. They rammed *Indianola* repeatedly until she had to be run aground near Grand Gulf to prevent sinking. Ironically, that very same day another steamboat named *Indianola*, a sternwheeler, hit a snag and sank just a few miles away.

Soon the Confederates attempted to repair and refloat USS *Indianola*, but abandoned her in a panic at word of the approach of more Yankee vessels, and the wreck sat on the bank for nearly two years before Federals finally refloated her in January 1865 and towed her to Mound City, where she was sold for scrap.

LANDING SUPPLIES ON THE JAMES RIVER

It is an ancient cliché of warfare that armies march on their stomachs. Many a general would attest that it is logistics – the management of men and supplies – more than strategy that wins campaigns. Never in history had warfare seen such a complex logistical challenge as that presented to the armies of the Union and the Confederacy during the Civil War. When single field armies numbered 100,000 or more, and with as many as three million men in service at one time or another, over a vast scene of conflict covering half the North American continent, the challenge of arming, equipping, feeding and clothing, and moving such armies was Herculean. Both sides met that challenge, though for the South it was always a case of trying to do too much with too little, especially as the Confederates lost control of the Mississippi and its major tributaries by 1863. Even had the South enjoyed command of the rivers, it never had enough steamboats to act as proper supply ships, and could ill spare those it had from conversion to armed vessels.

For the North, on the other hand, domination of the waters made it possible to shift men and material almost at will. Here on the James River in 1862, the bustle of the wharf reveals just a hint of the extent of what the paddlewheelers moved for Mr. Lincoln's armies. Mountains of boxes of hardtack – hard army bread – would have been seen beside massive piles of hogsheads of preserved meat, bales of fodder for the millions of animals that moved the wagons and artillery. Whole parks of cannon and quartermaster wagons and ambulances came off the steamboats. Everything from stationary to siege guns moved aboard Uncle Sam's transports, and the rivers allowed it to move to places to which neither railroads nor conventional roads – not to mention possible hostile Confederates in the interior – allowed access. It was an endless task, for an army on a single day could consume as much food and material as it took a score of heavily laden boats to move. Indeed, before a campaign, the boats worked overtime building up massive supply bases to enable a campaign to get under way.

The names of most of the transports are forgotten. Many of them never even had names, but only numbers painted on their stacks, yet their contribution to Union victory was inestimable.

STEAMBOATS AT PITTSBURG LANDING, 1862

Only a few days before this photograph was taken in April 1862, the first great battle of the Civil War fought in the western theater took place within a few hundred yards of this landing on the Tennessee River. The Battle of Shiloh was almost a disaster for the Union and for General U. S. Grant. Taken by surprise by the Confederate attack on April 6, he recovered and held out long enough for massive reinforcements to arrive on the opposite bank of the river, whence boats like these ferried them across to relieve his beleaguered divisions. The next day, April 7, Grant used those fresh troops to drive the Confederates back and claim victory. It was this river, striking as it did through the heartland of Tennessee and north Alabama, that Grant used to begin cutting the Confederacy in two, and it was command of the river with boats like these, bringing fresh troops and supplies, that made it all possible.

Grant's own headquarters boat the *Tigress* is tied up second from the right. She was just four years old, a sidewheeler that carried dispatches for Grant and which brought him from his land headquarters to the battlefield on the morning of April 6. A year later, when Grant sent his fleet past the Vicksburg batteries, she was one of the few boats lost to the enemy guns. Next to her at far right is the *Tycoon*, just two years old, first used as a troop transport for Grant, and now in service as a hospital boat for the Cincinnati Sanitary Commission, carrying supplies and medical materials for the wounded from the battle. Just months after the close of the war she was on her way north from New Orleans with 1,595 bales of cotton aboard when she caught fire north of Memphis due to sparks from her smoke stacks, and burned to the waterline.

On the other side of the *Tigress* sits the *Universe*, loaded with even more supplies for the Army and acting as a troop transport. Two years later she would be lost on the Mississippi when she hit a snag, further evidence of the constant hazard that accompanied all of these wooden vessels with their high pressure boilers, fragile bottoms, and a river highway constantly set with navigational hazards. Three other transports are tied up to the left, while the ghostly image of the timberclad *Tyler* is barely visible tied up on the opposite bank.

THE FLAG OF TRUCE BOAT
NEW YORK

Steamboats did more than take soldiers to war and bring them home again at the end of the fighting. Many served as headquarters for the ranking generals, one such being the *Tigress*, on which General U. S. Grant made his headquarters during the Shiloh Campaign, and of course Grant later used the *River Queen* in the last months of the war. Using a steamboat was not just a matter of the generals craving comfort or luxury. They also made for fast and ready transportation in times of crisis, as well as providing meeting rooms for councils of war, more secure from the elements and prying eyes than a tent in the woods.

Before long, paddlewheelers became virtual floating offices for any purpose required, and some branches of the United States government made them adjuncts of their land-based operations. Not only did the packets carry the military mail, but they also acted as post offices, hospitals, prisons, paymasters' offices, and more. They also came into use in the operation of the several cartels between North and South that attempted to deal with communications between the combatants. Places like Fort Monroe, Virginia, on Hampton Roads, became regular places for the exchange of information and negotiation aboard flag of truce boats. The same thing took place on the Mississippi. Most of all they were used as points of communication and exchange as the two sides traded prisoners of war in a system formally set up and operated through much of the war.

Here the flag of truce boat *New York*, a sternwheeler built in 1862 in Pennsylvania, is tied up awaiting one such prisoner exchange at Aiken's Landing, James River, Virginia, during the winter of 1864-65. Aboard the vessel, each Rebel prisoner being released from a Union prison had to sign his official exchange papers as he was traded for a prisoner from the Confederacy of equivalent rank. Thus boats such as the *New York* were happy places for released prisoners North and South, for it was here that their freedom from captivity was completed. The *New York*, though privately owned, was often employed by the United States during the war, carrying supplies and troops, and after the fall of Vicksburg she transported hundreds of captured cannon and other equipment north to Pittsburgh. Indeed, she served right up to April 1865, as the war was coming to an end, when she ran aground. After the war she plied from New Orleans to Pittsburgh carrying a traveling circus before she was destroyed by fire in 1870.

Ask any army commander in the field to pick his favorite steamboat, and likely he would not even know a name, but likely it would be a vessel like the *Chickamauga* that he would select. These nondescript and long forgotten little paddlewheelers were the backbone of the Union supply effort west of the Appalachians. The Ohio and Mississippi Rivers were navigable to almost any steam craft built, but their tributaries could be much more narrow and shallow, much more prone to shoals and rapids that the big boats could not overcome. Where they could, the Union armies marched along a rail line to maintain a constant stream of the supplies that kept armies going, but somewhere along its chain of succor, almost every army had to depend on water transportation at some point.

This was especially true of the armies in eastern Tennessee and north Georgia in 1863-64. Chattanooga, where a Union army was besieged in late 1863, and which served as supply base for William T. Sherman's armies as he launched his Atlanta Campaign the following year, was wholly dependent upon the Tennessee River as a lifeline. It was on this river that scores of vessels like the *Chickamauga*, named for a battle fought just a few miles from Chattanooga, kept up their constant beat, bringing foodstuffs like these barrels of salt pork for the soldiers. Others arrived piled high with sacks of grain and flour, sometimes doubling as bulwarks along the decks to protect the hands from enemy fire from shore. Most of these little sidewheelers were hastily built by the government on the Tennessee itself, and were designed especially for its hazards. Once the war was over they would be sold to private concerns, or used as wharf boats in Chattanooga and Nashville, their glory days gone. Even these little boats were armed, usually with a small field piece on the bow like the deck cannon just visible on the *Chickamauga*. Her pilot house, very exposed to Confederate sniper fire from the shoreline, also reveals extra wood cladding to protect master and helmsman.

On almost every day of the year after November 1863, the banks of the Tennessee at Chattanooga and Bridgeport and Stevenson and other places along the river, would be lined with dozens of these picturesque little craft disgorging the life's blood of the armies before they sank into obscurity.

ADMIRAL ANDREW HULL FOOTE

Few of the commanders of the steam Navy achieved the sort of notoriety and public acclaim given to the generals leading the armies. Admiral David G. Farragut became the North's greatest naval hero, and Raphael Semmes the South's, but neither saw service on paddlewheelers. David Dixon Porter, Farragut's foster brother, spent most of the war on paddlewheelers and commanding paddlewheel fleets, but his success was due as much to crafty politicking – and backstabbing Farragut – as to his own ability. Probably the greatest naval commander in the river steam service was the much less famous Admiral Andrew Hull Foote, the first officer of his rank to die in service.

Foote came from Connecticut, and was fifty-five when the Civil War began. He actually started his education at the Military Academy at West Point, but left to go to the Naval Academy at Annapolis, Maryland, instead. Upon graduation he took his commission in the Navy and remained there the rest of his life, distinguishing himself in command of the sloop USS *Portsmouth* in action against the Chinese at Canton's Barrier Forts in November 1856. He also sailed the African coasts for several years suppressing the outlawed slave trade, and made himself somewhat unpopular with the Navy enlisted ranks with his stand in opposition to the standard issue grog ration.

On returning with the *Portsmouth* to her home port in August 1861, he was assigned to command the steam fleet being assembled on the Ohio, including the timberclads and tinclads, and the Eads gunboats as they became available, his assignment being to work with Grant in taking control of the Tennessee and Cumberland Rivers. It was Foote who actually captured Fort Henry on the Tennessee on February 6, 1862, before Grant could get into action, and then on February 14 Foote's fleet bombarded Fort Donelson on the Cumberland, and was badly mauled, Foote himself being wounded aboard his flagship the *St. Louis*. Undaunted, he stayed in command in the following months though on crutches, and fought in the action against Island Number 10 before he was forced by his health to relinquish command.

His actions won Foote promotion to the rank of admiral, and he recuperated while holding a desk command in Washington until the spring of 1863, when he secured a new command, the South Atlantic Blockading Squadron. He was on his way to assume the new post when he died on June 26, 1863, a great loss to the Navy and the Union.

THE ILL-FATED *SULTANA*

During the Civil War, the navies saw the smallest loss of life of any of the armed services, not only in raw numbers but also in percentage of men engaged. That made it all the greater the irony that, just as the war ended, a steamboat and her captain were responsible for the greatest maritime disaster in American annals, and one of the half dozen worst in recorded history.

The sidewheeler *Sultana* was built during the war at Cincinnati, launching January 3, 1863, at 660 tons. She was powerful, with four boilers and 25-inch cylinders with an 8-foot stroke. Her paddlewheels had a diameter of 34 feet with each of the paddles or "buckets" measuring 11 feet in width. She started plying the Ohio between Cincinnati and Wheeling, West Virginia, and then took a government contract for the run up the Cumberland to Nashville. Early in 1864, with the Mississippi now cleared of Confederates and safely in Yankee hands, *Sultana* began making the run to New Orleans. Thereafter she regularly steamed back and forth between New Orleans and St. Louis. On her last downriver trip to New Orleans in mid-April 1865, she brought the shocking news that President Abraham Lincoln had been assassinated, and along with it intelligence of the surrender of Lee's Army of Northern Virginia. Then she started back upriver.

Sultana was back at Vicksburg a week later, suffering trouble with her boilers, which were repaired while her captain, J. Cass Mason, contracted with the government to use her as a passenger boat to take homebound Union soldiers upriver to St. Louis. She was rated to carry 376 passengers, but the government was paying $5 a head, and Mason decided to cram as many as possible aboard. Finally, when *Sultana* was fully loaded, she carried 1,886 men, five times the allowed number, many of them prisoners recently released from the Confederate hell-hole stockade at Andersonville. Severely overloaded, she steamed northward, stopping at Helena, Arkansas, where her photo was taken, the decks bulging with men, and at Memphis on April 26. That evening when she left again, she got only a few miles upriver on a pitch dark night with a storm just commencing, when three of her boilers exploded in the predawn hours of April 27, and she burned to the waterline and sank. Of the men aboard, at least 1,547 perished, a greater loss of life even than that on the *Titanic*.

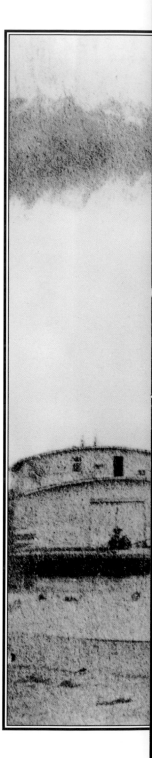

CAPTAIN THOMAS P. LEATHERS

Of all of the grand characters who populated the steamboat era, one man looms above all the rest, the formidable Captain Thomas P. Leathers. He generated more stories and legends than any other monarch of the rivers. His great home, Stanton Hall, still reigns as one of the finest of the Natchez mansions. Visitors to Vicksburg can still see in the Old Court House Museum the massive wooden rocker that he used in the pilot houses of his vessels, and later in old age at his home. And songs and stories and motion pictures and paintings for a century have celebrated his epic steamboat race aboard his own *Natchez* when he pitted her against the *Robt. E. Lee.*

Leathers had a special fondness for Natchez, as evidenced by the succession of steamboats he owned and captained by that name. His first *Natchez* was built in 1846, and he owned and operated her on the New Orleans to Vicksburg run for three years when he sold her and replaced her with the newly built sidewheeler *Natchez,* built in Cincinnati in 1849. He operated her until 1853 when he bought his third *Natchez,* nearly twice the size and tonnage of the last one, which he ran carrying up to 4,000 bales of cotton on the run between New Orleans and Natchez until she burned in 1854, killing Leathers's own brother in the blaze. Undeterred, he commissioned his fourth *Natchez,* which was almost exactly the same dimensions as the last one, put her to work in 1854 on the Mississippi between New Orleans and Vicksburg, and operated her until 1860. One of the few really successful owner-operators of steamboats, Leathers was already making himself a wealthy man, not least because he secured United States mail contracts worth $40,000 a year.

Leathers ran his latest *Natchez* until just before the outbreak of the Civil War, when he had sold her and she became a wharf boat in Baton Rouge. He had already commissioned the building of his fifth vessel, his biggest yet. Capable of hauling 5,000 bales, she started work in August 1860, but within a few months the start of the war ended the cotton trade on the river, and the Union naval blockade of the mouth of the Mississippi stopped almost all port trading in New Orleans. Leathers gave his friend Jefferson Davis a ride from Davis Bend to Vicksburg on the first leg of Davis's trip to become Confederate president, and afterward the *Natchez* carried the Confederate mail for a time. Reposing high confidence in Leathers, Davis offered him command of the Confederacy's makeshift river defense fleet, but Leathers turned it down, and instead operated the *Natchez* on the Whit and Yazoo Rivers before being forced to destroy her in 1863 to prevent her from falling into Yankee hands. He would have three more boats named *Natchez* in his colorful career, the next in line being the most famous of all. Incredibly, when Leathers died aged eighty in 1896, having survived everything the rivers could throw at him, it was because he was struck on the street in New Orleans by a man on a bicycle.

The *Natchez*
– A Real Winner

The combination of steamboats and the Mississippi was destined to be the spawning ground of legends, and the greatest story of all involved the sixth of Thomas P. Leathers's mighty *Natchez* boats, two of which are shown here. Having burned his last vessel in 1863 to keep her out of Yankee hands during the Civil War, he spent the next six years ashore, husbanding his badly eroded fortunes and waiting until he could get back on the river once more. By 1869 he could afford to commission a Cincinnati shipyard to build him another *Natchez*, one even bigger than her predecessors at 301 feet on the waterline, with a 42-foot beam, and massive engines powered by eight boilers. Still he had to scrimp in the austere days after the war, and the superstructure would have few of the frills and decorations that had adorned its predecessors. This was to be a working boat to rebuild his fortune and his domination of the river. When she first arrived in her namesake city in December, people were disappointed at her plainness, an editor describing her as looking like "a sick mule" tied to a board fence.

But Leathers knew his business, and at once began carrying cotton from Vicksburg to New Orleans in the season. Thanks to her spartan construction, she was light and fast, and in 1870 she set a new record for the upriver voyage from New Orleans to St. Louis. The prize was a set of deer antlers to display on her pilot house, beginning a tradition of antlers being given to the fastest boats or those that won races. Publicity over her lightning run led directly to the challenge between the *Natchez* and the *Robt. E. Lee* and the great race that commenced on June 30 from New Orleans to St. Louis. For day after day they steamed furiously north, the *Lee* ahead all the way, reaching St. Louis first after three days, eighteen hours, and fourteen minutes. The *Natchez* came in several hours later, but Leathers was not about to admit defeat. The *Lee*, commanded by Captain John Cannon, as formidable a character as Leathers, never stopped, taking on fuel while in motion, while the *Natchez* made several stops both for fuel and to take on and let off passengers. Thus, in actual steaming time, it took the *Natchez* less time to reach St. Louis than the *Lee*, but the debate over the victory would never be settled to everyone's satisfaction.

As for the *Natchez*, she worked on until 1879, when Leathers had her sold and dismantled to make way for his newest *Natchez*. This fell victim to an economic slump in 1887, then sank two years later, after which Leathers built his eighth and last *Natchez*, a smaller vessel that the elderly giant turned over to his son to command. In 1914 she was seized for debts, ending sixty-six years of Leathers skippers and *Natchez* boats on the rivers.

THE WRECK OF THE
T. P. LEATHERS

Besides running a series of boats named *Natchez*, Thomas P. Leathers was not at all modest about naming other vessels he owned after himself. The first *T. P. Leathers* was a sidewheeler built in Memphis in 1852, but she was a hard luck vessel that caught fire and was nearly lost in 1853, and finally left the river three years later. In 1885 Leathers built the second *T. P. Leathers*, this time a sternwheeler, in Freedom, Pennsylvania, and put her in service with his sons in charge, taking cotton from Vicksburg to New Orleans. Leathers himself oversaw some of her construction at the boatyard, but just five years after launch she sank a few miles above Natchez, thanks probably to being so overloaded with cotton that the water came over her gunwales.

Undaunted, Leathers built the third *T. P. Leathers*, another sternwheeler, at Jeffersonville, Indiana, in 1891. Leathers himself commanded her for a time, before old age forced him to turn her over to his sons. On October 22, 1896, shortly after the old man's death, she was coming downriver above Natchez, just like her predecessor, heavily loaded with cotton bales and sacks of cottonseed. In almost an exact replay of what happened to the earlier boat, water started coming in faster than pumps could handle it. Frantically the crew began jettisoning cotton bales and bags of seed, while the captain steered her toward the bank to run her aground and avoid sinking. She just made it, but for days afterward local sightseers and river passengers were treated to the sight of a near disaster. Hundreds of bales of cotton were floating down the river, or else bobbing in the water beside the beached *Leathers*, which had clearly taken in a lot of water, flooding her lower hull and ruining some of her machinery. Much of the cargo would be a loss to the insurers, while ironically, the Leathers family trademark on their vessels was a miniature bale of cotton displayed from the bows of their vessels.

The *T. P. Leathers* would be raised in spite of the disaster, at a cost of $12,000, and towed to New Orleans for repair and refitting, after which she stayed in service until 1900 when she hit a snag several miles above Natchez and this time went to the bottom, a total loss.

CAPTAIN JOHN W. CANNON

Born in June 1820, John W. Cannon started early in the steamboat business, buying the sidewheeler *Dallas* in November 1847, and the *Louisiana* in 1848, escaping the explosion on her that killed eighty-six people in one of the earlier and larger steamboat disasters on the Mississippi. He thereafter became a major stockholder in numerous steamboats, not just those that he captained personally. He brought out the sidewheeler *Vicksburg* in 1857, and the next year, after she made a record run, Cannon himself took her from Portland, Kentucky, down the Ohio, only to get into a fight at Paducah with a pilot who stabbed Cannon dangerously. In 1859 he took over the *General Quitman* on the New Orleans to Memphis run, and when the Civil War broke out he took her up the Red River and actually managed to keep her operating and out of Union hands for the balance of the war, after which he brought her back on the Mississippi and ran her until 1868, even as his success allowed him to buy part interests in several other vessels. In January 1866 he and Captain Thomas P. Leathers bought equal shares in the sidewheeler *Magenta*. In 1868, when Cannon sold the *General Quitman*, he conveyed a half share in the boat to Thomas P. Leathers, soon to be Cannon's greatest rival on the rivers, while Cannon himself began building the *Robt. E. Lee*, the vessel that would be forever linked in steamboat lore with Leathers's *Natchez*.

Cannon's long-time rivalry with Captain Thomas P. Leathers began in 1868 when the two got into an argument over the terms of charter of the sidewheeler *Belle Lee*, and there were stories of the two having a bitter fist fight on the streets of New Orleans that November. Cannon apparently got the better of the fight, which made Leathers all the more determined to win a few years later when their boats *Natchez* and *Robt. E. Lee* raced, though then, once again, Cannon emerged the winner, though not without continuing controversy.

One of the greatest of Cannon's boats was the resplendent *J. M. White*, built by Cannon and his partners in their Greenville & New Orleans Packet Company in 1878, but perhaps his greatest was his namesake *John W. Cannon*. She was a sidewheeler also launched in 1878, with some of the finest passenger accommodations ever seen on the river, catering exclusively to affluent travelers, including President U. S. Grant

Cannon was known on the river, despite his feud with Leathers, as a mild mannered and polite man, approachable and apparently without rancor toward anyone. Still, his life had been punctuated by some notable fights and feuds. Cannon was still owning and operating vessels as late as the 1880s until his death on April 18, 1882, near Frankfort, Kentucky.

THE COTTONBOAT
ED RICHARDSON

Many boats were designed for particular functions, whether it be to carry passengers, general freight, livestock, or a combination of all. Perhaps the most admired of all were the great cotton packets, their main decks designed to carry great weight, and wide enough to allow the stacking of hundreds of 500-pound bales. Virtually all were on the lower rivers, the Red and the Yazoo, and especially the Mississippi from Memphis down to New Orleans. Some owners specialized in them, and none more so than Captain John Cannon, owner of the famous *Robt. E. Lee,* victor in the controversial race with the *Natchez* paddlewheeler. The *Ed Richardson* was to be one of Cannon's finest cotton boats. He named her for a prominent cotton merchant in New Orleans who was also a planter near Greenville, Mississippi, and a pioneer in the growing business of deriving oil from cottonseed, otherwise a waste product of cotton ginning.

The *Ed Richardson* was designed as a sidewheeler and built at Jeffersonville in 1878, some 309 feet in length, with nine boilers and a main deck 95 feet wide to carry all the bales. She operated from January 1879, when Cannon himself rode her on her maiden voyage from Louisville, he and the rest of the passengers luxuriating in a main cabin that was 250 feet in length and 19 feet wide, with ceilings of more than 13 feet. When the *Ed Richardson* was in port, her massive twin stacks, with their turned tops and "feather" crowns, towered over the other vessels on the waterfront. She ran only until 1888, which was not much less than average life expectancy for a steamboat, yet she carried tens of thousands of bales of cotton in her time. That a steamboat could live such a short life before its owner decided to take it out of service is testimony to the money to be made quickly in the river trade before the railroads began to compete seriously. And more often than not, when a boat like the *Ed Richardson* was grounded, her metal work and finery, even her cabins, were often simply used to finish a newer vessel, as with this boat. She was dismantled and her hull burned in order to salvage her iron fittings, a sad end for one of the monarchs of the river.

PASSENGER ACCOMMODATION

The first steamboat of John Fitch, and the later Fulton's initial vessel, paid little attention to accommodations for passengers since it was anticipated that most of their trade would be people making simple day trips. The idea of a floating hotel was not so important on the Hudson and other eastern rivers, where distances were small and travel time relatively brief. But once Fulton and Roosevelt and Livingston began planning for the 1811-12 voyage of the *New Orleans*, it was inevitable that the operators should have to turn their attention to providing not just transportation, but also comfort, for trips that could last many days, even weeks. That first steamboat had just two cabins, one for the men and one for the ladies, the men's doubling as the dining room. The ladies' cabin, however, had some frills, including curtains and carpets.

Before long, however, builders began to take into account the needs of passengers for privacy. Soon every overnight packet offered at least a few state rooms for those who could afford the luxury of their own bed and a separate cabin, mostly married couples and ladies traveling alone or with their maidservants. Men traveling on their own would still often simply pay for deck space and sleep where they could. Gradually, however, the accommodations became more and more comfortable, until by the 1850s many steamboats were noted for their amenities. Few were ever very spacious. The grandest boats offered cabins only 8 feet by 10, or 9 feet by 12, but bedsteads and dressers or wardrobes became commonplace, with washstands and fresh water for washing provided by cabin attendants. Not until the twentieth century would full bathroom facilities become available, and even then not on all boats or in all classes.

Lacking ventilation or central heating, the cabins could be warm and stuffy in the summer, and cold in the winter, but operators managed to provide most of the comforts of a hotel room, only smaller. Where they could make up for it was in the dining rooms, which on some of the grander boats matched what was available in any of the best restaurants and hotels in New Orleans or Cincinnati. Thanks to frequent visits to New Orleans, Pittsburgh, and other major cities, the galleys had almost constant access to the best in seafood, wines, and more. If they could afford it, travelers could have almost anything available ashore. For the rest, most passengers brought their own food with them.

THE POKER GAME

Of all of the lore connected with the steamboats, perhaps nothing has captured the imagination quite like the legend of the riverboat gamblers. In fact, it is mostly legend. Few of the boats actually ran their own games or casinos, and very few of those who played cards or dice were actual professional gamblers traveling the boats. For a start, gamblers would have had to pay passage like any other traveler, whether they won or not, and more polite society looked askance at gamblers, an element that operators of the better boats would not want aboard their vessels. In fact, gambling aboard the boats was almost entirely an informal and spontaneous affair, a game gotten up at the suggestion of one or two gentlemen to while away the time on the water. Certainly stakes could be high, and no doubt some men lost their fortunes while a few others enjoyed spectacularly lucky days. But for the most part, it was entertainment and nothing more.

The legends would have it otherwise, however, and even before the Civil War there were already mythical tales appearing in the newspapers as fact, of daring and implacable card sharps on the boats. One of the most popular subjects was the celebrated James Bowie of Louisiana and Texas. Raised in the bayou country, a life-long entrepreneur in shady land claims and slave smuggling, Bowie was neither a notorious knife fighter nor a gambler. He was only in one verifiable duel – a brawl really – and yet soon was a legend as a fighter, while he was never known to gamble at all. Yet by the 1850s the tales of his winnings on the riverboats were everywhere. Usually they had him befriending some poor fool who had been cleaned out by a cheating sharp, whereupon Bowie would win back the man's losses and perhaps kill the gambler in the process. One tale widely believed even had him killing the equally legendary smuggler Jean Laffite.

But the scene shown here would be far more typical, though ladies would not have gotten into a game until late in the 19th century. Indeed, the absence of money or chips on the table suggests that they may just be playing for fun. Certainly, some men were better than others at the cards, but most of the real sharpers stayed ashore, content to let the suckers come to them in the "gambling hells" of Natchez-Under-the-Hill and New Orleans. It would be another century before gambling really became an important part of the riverboat experience, ironically a juxtaposition of traditions present today in a way it never was in the past.

THE RECORD BREAKING
JAMES HOWARD

A few of the boats became floating palaces, not many more so than the *James Howard*, known on the river by her nickname "Oil Cake Jim." Here was a magnificent vessel, indeed, 320 feet long, and a massive 53 feet in the beam. Built in 1870 at Jeffersonville, Indiana, she helped inaugurate the heyday of the grandest of the steamboats. Six massive boilers drove engines with cylinders almost three feet in diameter, while her sidewheels were each thirty-nine feet in diameter. Capable of carrying 3,200 tons, she cost more than $180,000 to construct. On her launch in 1870-71, she was thrown open to visitors to inspect, and an estimated 45,000 people walked her decks in a single day.

James Howard was put into the lucrative St. Louis to New Orleans run, specifically to carry cotton. Incredibly, she could carry as many as 7,701 bales on a single record breaking voyage in 1875, while other vessels eventually made that rise to 8,000. Yet she could still have room to treat passengers – many of then wealthy planters accompanying their crop – in the sort of style they enjoyed in their plantation mansions. The dining room served multi-course meals with the finest imported French wines, fresh oysters and seafood, while the social parlors featured small orchestras and gaming tables. State rooms boasted excellent attendant staff, gentlemen's horses could be accommodated, and even carriages could be transported for ladies and families. By the 1870s, as more and more planters emerged from the waste and impoverishment of the Civil War, the floating palaces like the *James Howard* became places to see and to be seen. The "Oil Cake Jim" even carried royalty, transporting Grand Duke Alexis of Russia and his companions down the river in 1872 to the February Mardi Gras in New Orleans, shortly before the Duke went farther west to go hunting in company with Colonel George A. Custer.

Yet the floating palaces faced the same hazards that dogged all steamboats. The *James Howard* was barely three years old when she caught fire off the Missouri shore and was scuttled intentionally to put it out. Unfortunately she sank in shallow water, and had to be quickly raised and towed to deeper water to be sunk again to stop the fire from consuming her. Raised and refitted, she worked another eight years before fire got her again at St. Louis in 1881 and destroyed her completely.

THE NO-FRILLS *MINNIE*

For every one of the great river steamers, there was at least another small boat, usually a sternwheeler, to bring the cotton or tobacco or livestock down the smaller tributaries to the ports like Vicksburg and St. Louis, as well as to take consumer goods back to the hinterlands. These smaller boats could simply pull ashore at a plantation landing, or steam up a bayou or even a wide creek, maintaining commercial and other contacts with the wider world. In Louisiana, especially, such boats hauled raw sugar cane from the plantations along the bayous to the refineries.

This little sternwheeler, the *Minnie*, shown here tied up at Natchez-Under-the-Hill, was built in Pennsylvania in 1869, and measured a mere 83 feet in length, by 18 feet in the beam, small indeed by steamboat standards. Captain Samuel Bell of Louisiana ran her on the lower Mississippi, where she operated on the tributaries for thirty years or more. She operated on such waterways as Loggy Bayou and the Minden, feeding inland cargoes to the larger boats bound for New Orleans. The photo shows an excellent portrait of a no-frills working sternwheeler of the era. The gingerbread is minimal, and restricted to the simple pilot house and a bit on the cabin deck. A few chairs line the cabin deck rail, either side of the boat's bell, but the chief impression is of a boat built for work. The main deck is almost completely open except for the machinery room aft, and the boilers forward beneath the pilot house. The cord wood piled about is evidence of the fuel constantly needed to keep her going, while the workman standing aft with a tool in his hand beside a pile of wood shavings and a timber propped on chairs, gives testimony of the constant upkeep and repair needed to keep any steamboat running. In the pilot house itself would be stood a proud man, perhaps Bell himself, or another pilot, while about the decks there would be the inevitable boys, perhaps dreaming of the day when they might themselves be pilot of a steamboat, even a little sternwheeler like the *Minnie*.

The *Minnie* herself made it to the turn of the century, a long career for any steamboat but, being smaller and less complex, she had less about her to go wrong. Moreover, her small draft of just over three feet made her and vessels like her far less susceptible to hitting snags and submerged hazards.

THE MAIL PACKET *CHESAPEAKE*

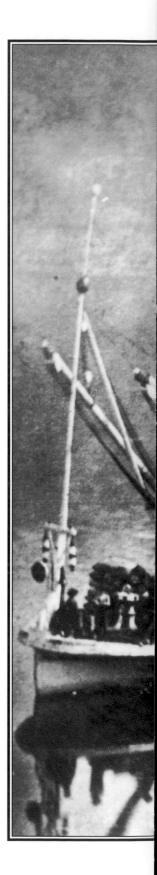

The term "packet" came to be applied almost generically to steamboats, but in fact it really referred only to those granted contracts for carrying the United States mail, including packages or "packets." Before the steamboat, mail delivery depended almost exclusively on overland routes by coaches and mail riders, a long, slow, and often uncertain means of communication. The steamboat offered a faster, and generally more reliable means of getting the mail to major points along the rivers, from which the coaches, and later the railroads, could get it to its destination. Few if any boats ever specialized exclusively in carrying the mail, but all companies sought contracts from the Post Office Department as an easy means of supplementing their regular business from passengers and freight.

The sidewheeler *Chesapeake* was a typical small packet, built in 1871 in Ohio. Though only 152 feet long, she was powerful. Her engine, which could turn her paddlewheels at a rapid twenty-eight revolutions a minute, could power her upstream at nine miles an hour, faster than most of the larger riverboats, making her one of the swiftest boats on the Ohio. Drawing only a little more than four feet of water, she could also pull into shore almost anywhere, as well as navigating tributaries, an important feature for a mail boat. She began running between Portsmouth and Guyandotte, but in 1873 was sold to the Parkersburg and Ohio River Transportation Company, and she appears here as she did when running mail and cargo for that company between Marietta, Ohio, and Parkersburg and Gallipolis, West Virginia. She stayed at that run for several years and then, as often happened, was replaced and sold to an owner who kept her in service on a more restricted run between Wheeling and Marietta. She appears here at a wharf on the Ohio, laden with sack goods, barrels, bales of animal fodder, and a variety of other freight, while passengers line her small cabin deck.

The poor *Chesapeake* did not meet a happy or glorious end. By the late 1880s she was reduced to being an excursion boat out of Pittsburgh, and in April 1887 was tied to the wharf when some youngsters as a prank started a wagon running down Market Street toward the boat. The wagon drove into the boat, and its tongue holed the hull below the waterline, sinking her before anything could be done to save her.

THE *CHARLES P. CHOUTEAU* – QUEEN OF THE COTTON CARRIERS

Steamboatmen were obsessed with records – the fastest run, the tallest or longest boat, the heaviest cargo. In an era before sports statistics captured the imaginations of young men and boys in America, everyone along the rivers knew which boats and which captains held all the really important records. The *Charles P. Chouteau* set and held one of the greatest of all.

She was built as the sternwheeler *Carondelet* in 1875 at Carondelet, Missouri, to carry freight alone, and with no frills. She ran cargo from St. Louis to New Orleans, and in January 1876 struck some submerged wreckage from a steamboat that had sunk some time before, and sank, losing much of her cargo. She was raised and was under tow to New Orleans for refitting and repair when a severe storm caught her and destroyed much of her remaining superstructure. There was nothing left to do but sell the hulk, and she passed through two or three owners before being repaired and put back in service, only to be badly burned in a fire in September 1877.

A captain from St. Louis bought the hulk and rebuilt her, and started carrying cotton from St. Louis to New Orleans. A year later he extended her hull an additional fifty feet and added cabins for passengers, generally improving both her appearance and performance, adding a custom made iron hull that gave her a nickname on the rivers as "Iron Charlie." The additional deck extension also made her, at 297 feet, the longest sternwheeler ever to ply the rivers until 1975 (there were many longer steamboats, but they were sidewheelers).

The purpose for that extra decking is evident in this photograph, taken near the end of 1878, for she was to be the queen of the cotton carriers. On one voyage in 1878 she carried 8,841 bales, a record exceeded only by one other boat, but in the single year 1881 she set her own record that remains unbroken, carrying a total of 76,950 in one season. As is evident, the comfort of passengers clearly took second place to cargo fares on such a run, for passengers would have to stand atop the bales themselves to see anything, and in summer such a dense packing could make the boat's interior stiflingly hot and humid. It was also dangerous, for any sparks could set all that cotton and hemp bagging ablaze, and that is exactly what happened to the *Chouteau*, when she caught fire, fully loaded with cotton, at Greenville, Mississippi, in November 1887, and burned to the water, a complete loss.

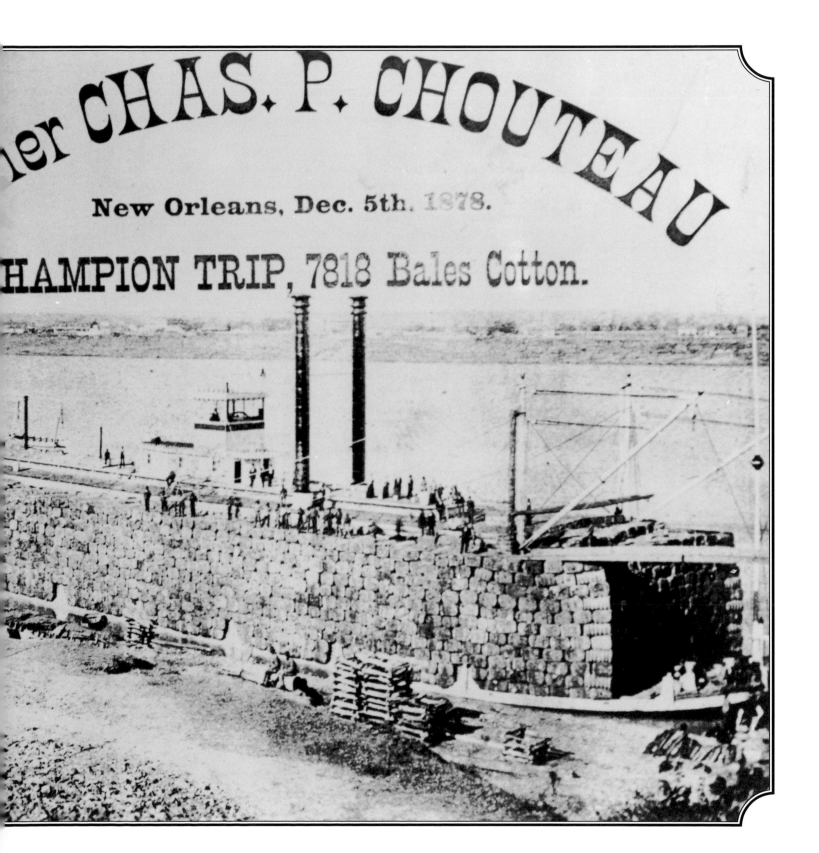

THE *FAR WEST* – CONVEYOR OF SAD NEWS

There was a special class of steamers called "mountain boats," that plied the waters of the upper Missouri and its tributaries, most notably the Yellowstone, boats like the *Far West*, the best known of them all. She was built in Pittsburgh in 1870, a sternwheeler dramatically smaller than the Mississippi and Ohio boats at only 190 feet in length and 33 in the beam, specifically to ply the narrower waters of those rivers. She had a main deck that was open to carry firewood and cargo, and a smaller cabin deck above with a dozen small state rooms and a main cabin for dining. She also had a daring captain in Grant Marsh, who was the only captain navigating on the Yellowstone – it was said he could steam on a heavy dew – and who took her up the river repeatedly for two years during the Sioux uprising in 1876-1877.

She made eighteen trips from Sioux City, Iowa, to Fort Benton, an eighteen-day journey, but surely her most famous exploit came in June 1876. On June 21, the day before orders put Colonel George A. Custer and his 7th United States Cavalry on the road to disaster in the hills overlooking the Little Big Horn River, Custer and others held a meeting aboard the *Far West* at the mouth of the Rosebud River where his assignment was discussed. That evening several of Custer's officers entertained themselves in a poker game aboard the steamboat, and left the next day. The *Far West* moved on up the Big Horn to supply the expedition, heading for the mouth of the Little Big Horn, which it reached on June 26, unaware that the day before several thousand Sioux and Comanche warriors surrounded and overran Custer and part of his regiment, killing them to the last man, and almost did the same to a separate party of the 7th that suffered heavy casualties but managed to hold out until relieved. The wounded were moved to the *Far West* three days later, and with her flag at half staff and her cargo mast draped in black, she started off for Bismark, South Dakota, making the 700-mile trip in a record time never afterward equaled. As soon as she touched the bank at Bismark, her crew rushed ashore to give the *Far West*'s melancholy news of disaster to the world. Her fame long outlasted the boat herself, which hit a snag and sank on the Mississippi in 1883.

THE LUXURIOUS *J. M. WHITE*

There had never before been a steamboat like it when the *J. M. White* came out of the Howard boatyard at Jeffersonville in 1878. She measured 321 feet from bow to stern, and 91 feet in the beam, with ten boilers to power huge 43-inch cylinders that drove two side wheels 43 feet in diameter. When she came off the ways on April 3, she was front-page news in nearby Louisville. Oak from West Virginia combined with pine from Pennsylvania, and special hardwoods from Indiana, to form a boat estimated at being capable of carrying 10,000 bales of cotton in a single run. Just the work of building and finishing the state rooms and passenger salons took up to forty men some ten months to accomplish, and required the invention of specialized machinery.

The appointments were wonderful. The whole interior design was built around luxury and comfort. Ceilings were high, chandeliers lit the main salons, and stained glass skylights lent color to the interior. Walnut and rosewood inlays and marquetry covered the paneled walls, while huge mirrors reflected light in the ladies saloon. There were two bridal suites that exceeded the scale of luxury of the rest of the boat. Passengers dined in a main cabin that was 233 feet long, carpeted and decorated with elaborate gingerbread, and lit by imported gilt chandeliers. She was not the largest ever built or the most elaborate, but somehow hers is the legend that has lasted. In her own time she was nicknamed "Mistress of the Mississippi."

She never got to carry that 10,000 bales, her record being just 5,067 due to a decline in the cotton business just at the time of her launch. The *J. M. White* made the New Orleans to Vicksburg run for nearly eight years, until the night of December 13, 1886, when a flame was seen in her cotton cargo. Within fifteen minutes of its being spotted, the blaze spread and engulfed the boat, and when it hit a cargo of gunpowder, the boat disintegrated. As many as twenty people lost their lives, and the cost of the loss of the boat and cargo exceeded $300,000. The greater price was the disappearance of one of the showpieces of the rivers.

ON DECK ON THE *J. M. WHITE*

One thing that the steamboats had in common with the ocean liners of their era and later was that the principal social venue was almost always the outer decks, weather permitting. Some paddlewheelers even had what they called "promenade" decks, virtual avenues where people went to see and be seen, providing sometimes a perpetual throng milling and strolling around the decks. It suited the era, a time when couples especially made an afternoon or evening stroll not only exercise, but a necessary social outing. Experienced steamboaters even developed a set routine involving circling one deck, then going down the stairs to the next, and so on, up and down the vessel. Those inclined to count could tally about a mile for every eleven times around.

Captains' chairs often lined the outer decks, as well as tables for writing or discreet cards – but never gambling. A water cooler on every deck made a refreshing drink available, while waiters were usually not far away if the passenger wanted something more. Sometimes, by informal accord rather than actual rules, men used one deck and ladies another. That the *J. M. White* specially catered for the comforts of male travelers is evident in this view of the magnificent cabin, with a spittoon every ten feet or so. On the other side of the walls it would be the same. Chairs would have been pulled back to the bulkhead to permit unrestricted room to promenade, but certainly a passenger was free to draw one out to the rail where he or she could best watch the river miles as they rolled past.

The state room doors opened directly out onto the decks, and there was nothing quite like stepping out of one's cabin after dark on a clear, starry, moonlit night, to watch the reflections on the glassy surface of the river, accompanied by the lulling swish of the paddlewheel and the faint sound of the draft through the tall stacks. Nothing could really detract from such moments, though on deck, as well as in the interior, there were always reminders of the hazards incumbent in any steamboat. On the wall would have hung an axe, about the only defense most early boats had against the ever-present danger of fire. Axes would not put out a fire, but in the absence of water hoses, they could help to contain fire's spread, and in the worst case allow deck hands to hack their way into a cabin to free passengers whose exit might otherwise be stopped by the flames.

THE *NEW MARY HOUSTON* – LIGHTING THE WAY

The naming of steamboats often seemed to challenge their builders and owners. Many became fond of a certain name, and used it again and again on a succession of boats. Thomas Leathers owned several named *Natchez*, and there were at least half a dozen named for Confederate General Robert E. Lee. Prefixes like "New" were very popular, even when the boats did not replace older vessels of the same name, but most often it denoted a replacement vessel. The original *Mary Houston* was built in 1868, but after nine years her owner wanted a larger boat and had her dismantled, selling the hull and keeping the machinery to power his *New Mary Houston*. Almost from the moment of her launch in 1877, she was a popular boat. She sat low and sleek in the water, 287 feet long, and when loaded with cotton, as she is in this picture, she ran with the river so close to her gunwales that the water often washed over her amidships deck, giving her the nicknames "Sloppy Molly" and "Dirty Moll."

The *New Mary Houston* represented an innovation in riverboating, for in March 1878 the owners installed a new electric search light that was the talk of the river. It could cast a beam as much as five miles ahead through the dark of night, giving better warning than ever before of oncoming traffic and obstacles. Soon electric lights would be the rule. The other amenities aboard made her one of the most popular passenger steamboats of her era, even though she was neither especially large or fast. Her round trip from Cincinnati to New Orleans and back could take twenty-five days, at a cost of $35, and yet she remained a favored boat.

Still, like almost all the great boats, her life was to be brief. She was almost lost in 1886 when moored above Louisville and a sudden storm carried her over the falls of the Ohio. Surviving that, she was not as fortunate seven years later when she was caught in a freeze at Cincinnati on January 10, 1893. A large ice flow broke loose upstream and came down, carrying the *New Mary Houston* away with it and driving her into a bridge pier with such force that the damage was irreparable. All that could be saved was her hull, which ended its days as an ignominious barge.

BUSTLING VICKSBURG IN 1883

Nothing speaks more of the bustle of the river waterfront than images such as this one taken in 1883 at Vicksburg. The bank was a scene of constant change, with packets coming and going daily, and vessels of every description in a jumble that made sense to boatmen but left landsmen utterly bewildered.

In the foreground the little packet *Le Flore* sits with cotton bales stacked up to her cabin deck. Built to operate on the Yazoo for the Parisot Line, she is clearly just arrived with a fresh load of bales to be transferred either to the rail line at Vicksburg, or else to a larger packet for the trip to New Orleans and the world's markets. She is tied to a flat topped hull, probably the razed remnant of a once proud steamboat now reduced to a floating wharf, while on the other side sits the Parisot Line's little sternwheeler *Sallie Carney*, said to be the first steamboat ever completely constructed at Nashville when she launched in 1876. She could act as a tow boat or tug, or could carry small cotton cargoes herself, operating short distances between Vicksburg and Davis Bend, once the home of Confederate President Jefferson Davis.

Behind the *Le Flore* sits the much more imposing *Will S. Hays*, her stacks still belching smoke as she is just in the act of arriving or leaving. She came off the ways at Freedom, Pennsylvania, in 1882 and was still gleaming new when the photo was taken. At more than 300 feet, she was one of the giants, with six boilers driving her massive engines. Moreover, she boasted electric cabin lighting provided by generators connected to her engines, and once set a record upriver passage from New Orleans to Cincinnati in six and one-half days, earning herself the sobriquet "Wild Bill." The tallest stacks in the center belong to the *Ed Richardson*, an even bigger vessel at 309 feet, with nine boilers and engines with 38-inch cylinders. She became one of the greatest cotton packets of all, yet lived only ten years before being intentionally burned to salvage her iron, an ignominious end to a great boat.

This was a scene itself not destined to last, for in a few years floods would change the course of the Mississippi, and Vicksburg would be left high and dry, while railroads would take over the cotton business once dominated by the steamboats.

PASSENGERS ON THE
CITY OF ST. LOUIS

So closely was St. Louis, Missouri, identified with the river and its traffic, that no fewer than ten paddlewheelers would bear its name over the years, including three dubbed the *City of St. Louis*. Two of them were simple sidewheeler harbor boats, one of which was later renamed the *Mark Twain* when the great author and one-time river pilot visited the city.

But the best known *City of St. Louis* was a sidewheeler built at Jeffersonville, Indiana, in 1883, a 300-foot-long giant with five boilers to power its engines and drive its 34-foot paddlewheels. She was built for the famous Anchor Line, whose trademark was an anchor suspended between the tall stacks of its boats. When the Anchor line fell on hard times, the *City of St. Louis* went up for sale by a United States marshal in 1898, and sold for a mere $19,000. She continued to pass through different owners, until 1901 when she wound up in New Orleans taking day excursions for passengers like these around the harbor.

This view, from the forward part of the boiler (main passenger) deck toward the paddle boxes, shows the pilot standing at left. He has just come off watch and has paused to talk with the ladies. Note also the wide guards (or extensions) beyond the boat's railing. Freight was piled on these guards if there was an extra heavy cargo. One important passenger in 1901 was President William McKinley.

Operating day excursions was a sad comedown for the once proud monarchs of the rivers, and yet by the turn of the century incursions from the railroad were starting to cut deeply into the river trade. Moreover, the paddlewheelers like *City of St. Louis* were expensive to maintain, especially wooden-hulled boats like her. Catering to the excursion trade would before long be almost the only way to keep them going, and that was seasonal, not to mention hazardous out of ports like New Orleans, which was already hosting huge ocean going merchantmen that used up a lot of channel, and sometimes moved too fast for a little steamboat to get out of the way.

The *City of St. Louis* avoided that fate, but ill fortune settled on her owners again all the same, and yet another United States marshal oversaw yet another sale for debt in 1903, this time for just $3,125. Taken back up the Mississippi one last time, her new owner tied her up at Carondelet, Missouri, and within a short time a fire broke out aboard her, and she burned beyond repair, quite possibly in order to collect insurance. No tally has ever been done of the number of paddlewheelers lost to fire over the years, but very likely as many as a third of them fell victim to flames.

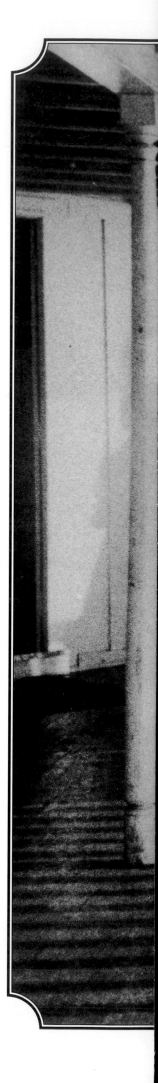

DINING IN STYLE

When that first steamboat *New Orleans* made its historic voyage down the Ohio and Mississippi in 1811-1812, one of its two cabins served as a dining room, but the fare was simple and prepared by the passengers themselves. That was a far cry from the experience enjoyed two generations later by the people who traveled the rivers, or at least by those who could afford passage in a state room, and meals in an elegant dining salon. On many vessels of the most stately sort, the main cabin doubled as the dining room. At meal times the settees and chairs were pulled back to the walls, and dining tables brought in and covered with Irish linen and fine sterling silver tableware. The diners ate off imported china, often decorated with the monograms and devices of the steamboat line, or even of the boat they were riding. Indeed, on many vessels the doors from the state rooms opened directly into the main cabin, meaning that a passenger could pass straight from dressing table to dining table.

Passengers ate breakfast between 7 and 10 in the morning, then a late lunch or "dinner" at 2 p.m., and then supper or a heavy tea around 7 p.m. or later, the meals spread out to help fill the day while under way. Thanks to the access that the river itself gave to sources of fresh seafood from New Orleans, and prime beef from St. Louis, the fare was outstanding, the talk of the continent. The finest imported wines were available, as well as fresh fruit and vegetables, and even ice cream. While deck passengers had to bring their own food with them and eat it cold, or else buy it at stops along the way, the full fare state room travelers enjoyed all the luxuries of a fine hotel, only on a slightly smaller scale.

This dining room on the Anchor Line boat *Belle of Memphis* reveals one of the more modest rooms, the diners seated in captain's chairs, each with the anchor device on its backrest. The service was attentive, the waiters virtually all black even in the days following the Civil War and emancipation, for steamboat service was one of the better jobs available to Negro men, while black women worked as chamber maids. Often a ladies' cabin stood at one end of the dining cabin, so that women passengers could retire from tea or a meal to a genteel conversation while the men stayed in the main cabin after the tables were removed and resumed their cigars and politics and card games.

Brennan
Photo.

WRECK OF THE *BELLE MEMPHIS*

The hazards awaiting any steamboat as they plied the rivers were almost too numerous to mention. The weather alone could turn against them. Rain could swamp a boat. High winds acted on the profile of a boat just as it did against a sail, and, if the pilot was unwary, could push the vessel sideways into the bank or some other danger. Shoal water and a rocky bottom could rip out a hull, while rapids like those at the falls of the Ohio at Louisville could drive her over rocks or into a tree-lined shore. Tornadoes could disintegrate a steamboat, while any number of manmade hazards came aboard with every passenger. Careless cigars most likely burned as many steamboats as boiler fires.

The greatest danger at first were the innumerable snags. The Mississippi and its feeder tributaries are a gigantic waste system, carrying everything that falls into the water from Montana to Pennsylvania, down its waters. As banks caved in by erosion or storms, uprooted trees floated downriver, and at some point often sank, waterlogged, to jam themselves fast into the bottom mud, often submerged from sight. Because of the way they sank, they usually settled with their tops pointing upstream, the force of the water only fixing them tighter. When a boat ran onto one, coming downriver especially, it could rip out her bottom. Then there were the "sawyers," trees less firmly fixed in the mud. The current would periodically lift their upper ends out of the water, before the weight of the tree took over and sent it crashing back down with a loud splash. A sawyer could be just as dangerous as a snag, and between them they accounted for the majority of the hundreds of steamboat wrecks.

The *Belle Memphis*, one of the pride boats of the Anchor Line, had a fine pedigree, that included Horace Bixby serving a stint as her pilot, the same man who taught the river to Mark Twain. She actually escaped a May 1896 tornado that destroyed two other Anchor boats, the *Arkansas City* and the *City of Vicksburg*, but then the poor boat struck a snag on the upper Mississippi in September 1897, and was reduced to a broken-backed complete loss.

FIRE DOWN BELOW

The greatest fear aboard a steamboat was fire. After all, when running, every paddlewheeler had anywhere from one to half a dozen furnaces blazing, any one of which could spread its flames to anything flammable carelessly left within reach. Then there were the glowing cinders spewing out of the stacks. Theoretically, the heat and updraft of the smoke from the furnaces would carry any such sparks safely above and aft of the boat before they could settle on a wooden deck or land on a cotton bale, but in practice just the opposite happened with regularity. Then there were the boilers, which could overheat and explode, or burst a defective seam, and themselves blow sparks and cinders from the furnaces all over the engine deck. And on the passenger boats there were almost always galley fires cooking meals and heating the water for coffee and tea, not to mention perhaps hundreds of male passengers smoking their pipes, cigars, and cigarettes, and any one of them could drop a glowing ash onto a deck, or down among the cotton bales and freight.

Add this to the danger from snags, sawyers, collisions with bridges and piers, not to mention other steamboats, and the wonder, indeed, is that not more boats succumbed to such misadventure, but the number was high enough. In just a brief alphabetical rundown of a dozen steamboats, the sad tale of accidental ends is plain enough: *Freestone*, snagged and sank in 1865; *Freighter*, bottomed out on the Red River and sunk, 1859; *French*, lost to fire in 1914; *Friendly*, burned 1892; *Frolic*, burned 1849; *Frontier City*, sank in 1861; *Fulton*, hit a snag and sank in 1849; *Fulton City*, snagged and sank in 1858.

As a result, photographs like these of paddlewheelers burned, blown apart, or settled on the bottom, their backs broken, their cargo spilled into the river or lost, became commonplace in the great steamboat era. Indeed, one of the greatest local spectator attractions, next to the majestic beauties themselves, was the sight of one of them at her sad end. Locals brought picnic lunches to eat beside the wreck, while scavengers and little boys picked through the ruins for souvenirs before the professional salvagers got to the scene. From birth in shipyards right through to their sad, often squalid death, the steamboats dominated the attention and imagination of the river people.

THE *DUBUQUE* AT DUBUQUE

There is something poignant, not to mention portentous, about the image of the plucky little *Dubuque* passing the swinging bridge of the Dubuque Railroad tracks at their namesake Iowa city. Even though both steamboats and railroads came into being in America at almost the same hour, still the one was resilient and flexible enough to go almost anywhere, while the other was forever tied to the rivers, meaning that vast areas of the continent could never be served by the paddlewheelers. Inevitably, time and expansion and development would mean that the railroad must prevail. In a way it was the old and the new side by side here in Dubuque.

There had been several *Dubuques*, the first built in 1847, only to sink in the Mississippi eight years later. Another was built in 1867, and was the pride of its fleet, with specially commissioned landscape paintings decorating its main cabin, but she had an accident – ironically with a railroad bridge pier – on her maiden voyage, and burned in 1879. The *Dubuque* shown here, beside her namesake's old nemesis, a railroad bridge, was built at Cincinnati in 1879, and was first called the *Pittsburgh*. She was a hard luck boat, too, losing her upper decks in a tornado in 1896, when she was rebuilt as the *Dubuque*. Then in 1901 she struck a snag that tore a 140-foot hole in her bottom, sinking her. She was raised and put back in service, but had yet another rendezvous with destiny and railroads when in 1914 her captain had a heart attack and died at the wheel just as she was approaching a railroad bridge at Alton, Illinois.

In fact, railroad bridges represented a constant hazard to steamboats, and continued to do so from the time of the construction of the very first span across the Mississippi, the Eads Bridge at St. Louis, down to the present. Moreover, as the rivers came more and more under control of the Army Corps of Engineers as they dammed the streams to control flooding, and installed locks for the boats, every such new construction represented an additional danger. Even within the last few years, as the remaining passenger steamboats on the rivers enjoy the most modern navigational aids, there are still occasional collisions with bridge piers and lock walls, and probably there always will be. Only a fool, then or now, takes the river for granted.

THE *QUINCY* AT ST. LOUIS

St. Louis saw its first steamboat in 1817, and thereafter it became one of the most bustling river cities in the nation. It served as a virtual hub for all upper Mississippi traffic, as well as a gateway to the Missouri. Moreover, when the railroad reached St. Louis in the 1860s, the city linked the rails to the water, further helping to open the continent. By the time of the Civil War it was one of the largest cities in the nation, and by the turn of the next century ushered in a host of innovations, from widespread use of electricity, to the hot dog. It was also home port to a number of steamboat lines, probably the best known being the Streckfus Steamers, who were a presence on the Mississippi for decades.

The city's waterfront appears here at about that time, in 1903, row upon row of warehouses, commission houses, and merchants, beneath a skyline that betrays a growing industrial city. On the river itself the Diamond Jo Line's sidewheeler *Quincy* floats tied up to a wharf boat, with a coal barge alongside for her to take on fuel for her furnaces. Built in 1896 on a hull that came from one salvaged vessel, engines from another, and her upper cabins from yet another broken up steamboat, the *Quincy* made the upriver run from St. Louis all the way to St. Paul, Minnesota, with principal stops in Davenport, Iowa, and other cities along the way, and continued doing so, even after she sank in 1906 off the Wisconsin shore, and had to be raised.

Joseph Reynolds, the "Diamond Jo" owner of the boat, sold all of his vessels in 1911 to the Streckfus Line of St. Louis, and *Quincy* become the pride of the Streckfus fleet. She began steaming to New Orleans, with extra cabins constructed on her Texas deck to accommodate the demand for passenger space. In fact, she would be the last sidewheeler to make the St. Louis-New Orleans passage on a regular basis. In the end, just after the end of World War I, Streckfus converted all of its boats to excursion vessels to take charters out on the river for dinner and dancing, and the *Quincy* was reconfigured into the *J. S.*, and operated as a day excursion boat for several more years.

The number of men needed actually to operate one of the paddlewheelers was rather few, considering the size of some of the boats. Over all stood the captain, or master, who might have been sole owner of the boat as well, or a partner, or just another employee. He might also act as pilot when he wished or when needed, but on many boats he was more of an executive with ultimate responsibility for everything that happened aboard. A pilot actually steered the vessel, and some specialized only on certain portions of the river, meaning that on a long voyage from Pittsburgh to New Orleans, for instance, a boat might take on one pilot after another as it progressed. A first mate oversaw day to day operations on larger boats, with a succession of mates below him depending on the size of the vessel. A chief engineer oversaw the engine room, with as many mates and stokers as necessary to keep the boilers fired and the engine running smoothly.

This was all that was needed actually to operate the boat, but many more men worked on them. There were always roustabouts and deck hands for everyday chores, and to help with loading and offloading cargo, though much of that work, then as now, was done by day laborers hired in port. On the passenger vessels of any size there had to be a few state room attendants, and if there was a dining room, then that called for cooks and waiters. With the exception of the pilots and chief officers, and the engineers, few of the boatmen had to be specially skilled for their work, and most could learn on the job, while the cabin and dining room staff often came straight from hotel and restaurant jobs ashore.

The deck hands were perhaps the most colorful, and certainly the rowdiest. Some vessels achieved reputations for their boisterous crewmen, who blew off steam when they came ashore in places like Natchez-Under-the-Hill and not infrequently drank and gambled and fought too much for the good name of their profession. In cities like New Orleans and St. Louis, whole waterfront sections of town were considered off limits for polite society, where the boatmen held sway. Yet most were simple workmen as in any profession, though theirs had about it a worldliness and romance they would never have found ashore, one reason that they stayed at their professions for years, proud of the aura that surrounded being a "riverman."

THE *SPRAGUE* – A RIVER WORKHORSE

Not all steamboats were passenger or packet vessels, of course, and the biggest of all was a Mississippi River towboat, something of a misnomer since on the river towboats do not "tow," but push their cargo in barges, several of which tied together are called the "tow." Nothing on the river ever compared to the great *Sprague*, built in 1902 at a cost reputed to be half a million dollars. Instead of wooden construction, she was built almost entirely of steel, something not seen on the rivers, and many an old hand warned that a steel boat would be too rigid to "flex" and "bend" with the water. Her massive stern wheel stood thirty-eight feet high, and at first she did, indeed, appear to be jinxed. On her maiden voyage she collided with a showboat, and revealed an alarming number of design defects that had to be corrected when she reached New Orleans after her first trip.

Nevertheless, *Sprague* proved the skeptics mistaken, for she became a river workhorse for the next forty-six years, an unusually long career for any steamboat. Nothing on the river could push larger or heavier tows, and rivermen soon came to call her "Big Mama." In the face of increasing competition from railroads, a monster like *Sprague* could move barges carrying the equivalent of 1,575 rail cars of cargo in a single "tow," and right up to the present the tonnage carried on the Mississippi and its tributaries dwarfs that moved by rail and truck. A single barge can carry the capacity of dozens of eighteen-wheel semi-trucks, and at considerably less cost.

Even when she was taken out of service in 1948, *Sprague* was still capable of continuing her career, but newer and faster tow boats dominated the rivers by then, and she had become an anachronism. Finally she was simply beached on the Mississippi shore, where she became a landmark for the next thirty years, her bright red paddlewheel and rusting stern clearly visible to passing vessels. Gradually she decayed, subject to vandals and floods and overgrowth, until the hulk was dismantled after a heavy flood broke her up. Still part of her remains, as some of her paddlewheel and machinery, as well as her nameplate, have been preserved in a Mississippi River steamboating museum.

PRESIDENT TAFT'S FLOTILLA

Perhaps there was no grander, or more unusual, sight on the rivers than an actual flotilla of steamboats. As a rule, they did not travel in groups, there being no need to do so, and the proximity of several boats steaming together actually represented something of a navigational hazard not only to themselves but to other vessels. But in October 1909 such a "fleet" was seen on the Mississippi as it brought President William Howard Taft downriver from Memphis to attend the so-called "Lakes to the Gulf Deep Waterways" convention in New Orleans, organized to encourage and foster the future use of the rivers for transportation and commerce.

In fact, it was quite a company, including not just the president, but a number of Congressmen and senators, and more than one state governor, as well as a few representatives of other nations. Vessels representing all kinds of paddlewheelers formed the flotilla. Taft himself traveled aboard the *Oleander*, a United States Lighthouse Service tender used ordinarily to maintain and service navigational lights placed along the rivers for greater safety. The *Oleander*, a six-year-old sternwheeler, is tied up third from the right, amid the rest of the flotilla, on October 29 during their stop at Natchez, Mississippi. In all, fully a dozen steamboats crowd the landing at Natchez-Under-the-Hill, all of them bedecked with bunting and flags, while the empty coal barges beside them testify to full fuel bunkers aboard ship for the remaining day's trip on to New Orleans.

No president had ever traveled the river in such style or panoply before, and very few had actually used the rivers when in office at all. Andrew Jackson was the first president to make the trip down the Mississippi by paddlewheeler, but that had been in 1828, ten months before his election. For Taft, the whole journey represented a juxtaposition of old and new transportation. A train had taken him to Memphis, then the steamboat down river, and a procession of automobiles brought him from the river to a ceremony on the bluffs. It all seemed to indicate that, with the new century just in its infancy, the government and business were uniting in anticipating a prosperous future for steamboating. Nevertheless, like most of their sisters, the vessels in this flotilla did not meet glorious or happy ends. The *Oleander* herself would wind up being dismantled and her hull used as a coal barge, an ignominious fate for a boat that once had been "Steamboat One."

THE DAY EXCURSION

Almost from the first, steamboats were seen not just as transportation for freight and passengers, but also as means for having a "day out," a pleasant river trip for its own sake. Indeed, many of the passengers on John Fitch's first operating steamboat in 1790 were simply making the trip up or down the Delaware as a novelty, and the same would be the case with Fulton's *North River Steamboat of Clermont* years later. Once steamboats became a practical reality, however, and especially on the Ohio and Mississippi, where the distances were great and only really practical for commercial or serious travel, excursion steamboating was confined chiefly to the Atlantic seaboard rivers, especially New England and the mid-Atlantic.

But by the dawn of the twentieth century, as the railroad took over more and more of the carrying trade, taking passengers to places hundreds of miles from the nearest navigable river, and cargo to and from spots not serviced by water, use of the steamboats for practical personal and business conveyance rapidly began to disappear. By World War II and the universal spread of the automobile, it had all but ceased entirely, and the last of the overnight packet boats disappeared from the great rivers. In their place, the excursion boats emerged, returning steam to one of its earliest functions. Special boats were built for day excursions and dinner cruises out of ports like Louisville and New Orleans, while other older boats that had been freight boats, even car ferries, were converted, to entertain new generations of Americans who felt a longing to return to steam not from necessity, but nostalgia.

Many packets were converted by companies specializing in the new tourist trade. Decks that once held automobiles were turned into dining rooms. Cabins no longer needed were removed to created dance halls, and calliopes – which rarely ever appeared on steamboats in their heyday – were introduced to amuse passengers. Instead of steaming from port to port, the new vessels simply made brief round trips of an hour or two. Rather than coal or wood fired boilers, their engines were driven by oil, and in a final insult, several vessels had their steam plants removed entirely, to be run by gasoline and diesel-powered propellers, while the paddlewheels were turned merely for nostalgic effect.

Today, while several excursion boats operate on the rivers, there are only three overnight steamboats operating on the Mississippi and its tributaries, all catering exclusively to an affluent tourist market, and carrying neither freight nor passengers traveling just for transportation. And yet, more and more new paddlewheelers are being built for the new trade, showing as so often before that the steamboat can adapt with the times and changing demands to remain a permanent part of the American landscape.

THE DE LUXE *J. S.*

Some steamboats had multiple incarnations on the rivers. One such was the *J.S.* Her origins went back as far as the *Alex Mitchell*, a sidewheeler built in 1870 at Paducah, which spent most of its career on the upper Ohio and upper Mississippi before she was dismantled in 1881. Builders took her engines and machinery and upper cabin and used them to complete the *Gem City*, then being fitted out at St. Louis, to travel the upper Mississippi. Sold in 1891, her new owners rebuilt her four years later at Dubuque, Iowa, to run between St. Louis and St. Paul as the *Quincy* for the Diamond Jo Line. The *Quincy* would continue to work for twenty-one years, occasionally making the run all the way to New Orleans. In fact, she was the last sidewheeler ever to make the trip from St. Louis to the Crescent City. Over the years she sank once in July 1906 when she hit a snag in the upper Mississippi, but had managed to run into shore so that all her passengers got safely away. Soon she was raised and put back in service, and finally became the property of John Streckfus and his company, Streckfus Steamers. She was the pride of the Streckfus fleet, which continued to add passenger cabins onto her upper deck to accommodate demand.

By 1917, Streckfus decided that the *Quincy* could no longer handle the business, but he refused to abandon a boat that had meant so much to the company and the river. Instead, he decided to give her yet another incarnation. After extensive rebuilding, she emerged as the *J.S.*, pridefully given her owner's initials, themselves borrowed from a previous boat that had burned in 1910. She was completely rebuilt on the *Quincy*'s hull at Dubuque, and then put to work carrying passengers out of St. Louis for another fifteen years. After that she plied the upper Ohio, largely taking excursion parties, until finally she was taken out of service and dismantled at St. Louis in 1939. She was an impressive sight on any water, her ornate pilot house towering above her teeming decks. People on the banks often called her the "J. S. De Luxe," thanks to the ornate words painted on her sidewheel paddle boxes. Amazingly, some of her machinery and cabin work had lasted in operation for almost seventy years.

PILOT HOUSE OF THE *CAPITOL*

This was the virtual kingdom of the steamboat captain and pilot, the realm in which he was undisputed master of all he surveyed. From this Olympian place, though only a deck or two above the passengers and crew, he was truly the master of his world. It was a simple, even Spartan domain. His "throne" could be nothing more than a simple rocking chair, rockers being somehow traditional seating on steamboats, though Tom Leathers's gigantic chair certainly stood out above the others. This one was far more common. This monarch had no sword or scepter, but instead he held in his hand the two great controls that managed his kingdom. The ship's wheel was enormous, dwarfing the rest of the room in a way, so large on most boats that half of it extended below the deck. In large part the size was to provide enough mass that turning would be easier, since the wheel was connected to the rudders by ropes and pulleys, and a smaller wheel would not have had the leverage needed to do the job. The size also allowed for very subtle shifts in course that would have been almost impossible with a smaller wheel.

The other vital control was the "telegraph" at right, virtually identical to those found on ocean going steamers, and scarcely changed even well into the last century. With it the pilot could signal to the engine room a stop, or reversal, or increase or decrease in speed. The *Capitol* being a newer vessel, there was also a telephone on the wall above the telegraph for more precise communication. Otherwise, this throne room was a working place, unornamented, fitted with little else but an overhead rope for ringing the ship's bell and steam whistle, and a small cabinet for charts.

The *Capitol* had in fact been converted in 1920 from the older Streckfus sternwheeler *Dubuque*. She needed that large wheel, for she carried four main rudders and two additional "monkey" rudders for steering her 256-foot bulk. Even though her career came only after the glory days of steamboating, working out of St. Louis and New Orleans as an excursion boat like the rest of the Streckfus line until she was finally dismantled in 1945, still when he stood at this wheel, her captain could yet feel the ancient lure of the river, and the pride of being in command.

THE *ADMIRAL* EXCURSION BOAT

Probably the strangest looking steamboat ever built was one of the last, an almost surrealistic blend of past and future that reflected the complete dominance of the excursion trade in the twilight of steamboating. She began as the *Albatross* in 1907, an undistinguished sidewheeler designed and built at Dubuque for the Louisiana & Mississippi Railroad Transfer Company as a vessel for the Vicksburg and upriver trade, and capable of taking sixteen loaded railroad cars aboard as well as a little conventional cargo. She almost never made it to Vicksburg after her launch, thanks to near disaster on the Mississippi that could have seen her driven into a bridge, but she narrowly escaped. In 1920 she was lengthened, and continued to work until she was on the lower Mississippi in 1937 when Streckfus Steamers bought her to refit and replace the aging *J. S.* The principal attraction of *Albatross* was her strong steel hull, capable of carrying loaded boxcars and therefore able to sustain the heavy new superstructure that was planned.

The new owners spent almost two years at the shipyard in St. Louis converting *Albatross* into the excursion boat *Admiral*. She was almost all steel, from her hull to her superstructure, capable of taking up to 4,400 people on day cruises on the Mississippi from home port. Her exterior design represented the futuristic ideas recently displayed at the New York World's Fair, a blending of Art Deco and Flash Gordon. Gone were the trademark tall stacks, and even the paddlewheels were completely enclosed. The result was a boat designed completely for function, with the lore of the steamboat all but forgotten. Whatever she lacked in traditional ambiance, however, she made up for in comfort, being the first excursion boat on the rivers to have air conditioning, a revolutionary innovation when she carried her first day-trippers in 1940. The *Admiral* continued taking thousands on excursions out of St. Louis until 1974, when her steam engine and boilers were removed, as well as her paddlewheels, and replaced with diesel engines and propellers. Thereafter she continued to operate until 1979, when her seventy-year-old hull could no longer pass Coast Guard requirements, and she was taken out of service and permanently tied up not far from St. Louis's famous Gateway Arch. Remodeled into a restaurant and party center, she remained a familiar sight on the St. Louis waterfront, and yet a sad reminder that the great days of the steamboats were gone.

MODERN STEAMBOAT RACES

Put a man on or in anything that can move, and sooner or later he will be compelled to pit it against another man in competition. Racing of steamboats was inevitable. No one knows when the very first one took place, but very likely it was a spontaneous and informal affair that occurred simply when two boats bound in the same direction came abreast and the pilots or captains yelled a challenge to each other. There was even more impetus for racing, of course, in the very nature of the steamboat business, since a part of the advertising lure of many boats was their power and thus their speed between ports. Indeed, apart from accommodations or capacity, really the only choice to be made between one vessel and another was its schedule and its speed. Thus racing was good publicity – for the winner – and could translate into advanced prestige on the river, and more business. For some men, of course, racing became more. Thomas P. Leathers and John W. Cannon used their great race as one of a series of contests in a long history of angry competition and confrontation between them.

Steamboat racing disappeared with the old boats themselves, but it has come back to the rivers thanks to the modern overnight passenger sternwheelers *Delta Queen*, *Mississippi Queen*, and *American Queen*, and the *Belle of Louisville*. Years ago a tradition of an annual race between the *Delta Queen* and the *Belle of Louisville* began, the prize being a set of golden antlers, just as in the 1800s a pair of antlers represented the victor. The antlers have passed back and forth between the two boats, and quite a tradition of pilots' tactics, even tricks, has come to be associated with the good-natured event, one such shown in the main picture here, taken in 1972, while the smaller photo shows the start of a race between the Cincinnati and America in 1929 in the Louisville harbor. Meanwhile, the overnight paddlewheelers occasionally race among themselves, sometimes, just as in the old days, without prior arrangement, but simply when one overtakes the other, and then both pile on the steam. Of course, today's passengers run none of the risks of those of yesteryear, who faced the possibility that in his anxiety to crown more steam and speed, a captain might blow his boiler or even wreck his vessel, with potentially tragic consequences. Today's steamboat races are spectator events, fun for all, in a rivalry that is friendly yet reminiscent of one of the great experiences of the steamboat era.

THE GAMBLING BOATS

Myth and folklore have always associated gambling with the riverboats, but card games and casino style gambling was never as ubiquitous on the paddle-wheelers as legend suggests. Still, what there was of it had disappeared on all but an informal basis well before the overnight steamboats themselves died out, discouraged by local laws in the states through which the boats passed, and by changing mores in a post World War I generation of prohibition. By the post World War II years, with gambling outlawed everywhere in the nation except Nevada, riverboat gaming was only a nostalgic memory kept alive in motion pictures and historical novels.

By the 1970s, however, new pressures and changing attitudes encouraged a resurgence of legalized gaming, first at Atlantic City, and then on Native American reservations which were given special exemption from anti-gaming laws. Inevitably someone would have the idea of bringing gambling back to the rivers. As it happened, many of the states with the greatest connection to the rivers, states like Mississippi and Louisiana, Missouri and Indiana, were also most in need of an economic boost without resorting to taxing an already hard-pressed citizenry. Without removing the restrictions on gambling entirely, these states enacted laws to grant special licenses for casinos to operate on the water, and the riverboat theme was a natural.

By the 1990s a score or more of water casinos appeared from Gulf Shores, Mississippi, to Baton Rouge and Vicksburg, Natchez, Tunica, St. Louis, and more. Ironically, some of them are not true riverboats at all, but merely floating casinos tied permanently to wharves. Some are not even boats, but stand fixed immovably to the bottom. A few, however, genuinely operate on the waters around their home ports, some being required by law to be able to act like true boats, and thus they take their gamblers on hour-long excursions up and down river, but there is little involvement with the trip, for the attractions on these boats are the tables and the machines and the restaurants and shows within. While some have vestigial paddlewheels, almost all are driven by propellers powered not by steam but by diesel engines. The irony is that there never was in the past such a thing as a gambling boat. Gaming was simply something that people did while traveling, but to a modern generation of Americans these stylized vestiges combining two old traditions are all they may ever know of a once great era on the rivers.

THE "TALL STACKS" FESTIVAL

The inescapable lure of the river and the steamboats that once dominated its life and people finally brought thousands together in a celebration of the era. In October 1988, as part of the bicentennial of the city of Cincinnati, which has always had such a close association with the boats, a festival called "Tall Stacks" was inaugurated. Fourteen riverboats came to the event, from authentic steamboats like the old *Delta Queen*, to modern reproductions used in the excursion business, from cities up and down the Mississippi and Ohio. The event proved such a success that four years later another "Tall Stacks" was held, and another in 1995, and yet another in 1999. The event is now firmly fixed as part of Cincinnati's celebration of itself, and the rivers.

Lasting up to five days, the festival features riverboat cruises on all of the boats attending, steamboat races, lectures, calliope concerts, and non-stop entertainment representing the music of the rivers and their cultures. There are lectures and workshops, and more than a hundred acres of outdoor exhibits at which collectors display steamboat memorabilia and rural craft activities. Even Civil War reenactors get into the act, and scores of people in period costume walk the streets and waterfront giving living history demonstrations of tall tales and famous river characters. For those who like noise, there are also demonstrations of steam whistles, whose shrieks echo along the banks of the Ohio.

In 1999 some nineteen riverboats made the journey to Cincinnati, representing every description of vessel, from the authentic sternwheelers *Belle of Louisville*, *Delta Queen*, *Mississippi Queen*, and *American Queen*, to "ornamental" sidewheelers like the little *Anson Northrup* from Minneapolis, or the even smaller *Spirit of Cincinnati*. But they are all paddlewheelers, and their lure is such that nearly one million people came to see them.

A special feature of "Tall Stacks" is the annual pitting of the *Belle of Louisville* against the *Delta Queen*, for the coveted golden antlers. All of the boats attending are open for tours, and they take turns providing river cruises. Even the surrounding communities get into the spirit, making "Tall Stacks" not just a city event, but a regional festival. No sooner is one "Tall Stacks" concluded than already the people of the river and paddlewheel enthusiasts everywhere begin looking forward to the next as they keep alive the spirit and excitement of the steamboat era.

THE THREE QUEENS

By the 1940s, many people believed that the day of the grand paddlewheeler was done, that their majestic profiles would never be seen again on the rivers, and that the evocative sound of the steamboat whistle had echoed its last. But they were to be proved wrong. Shortly after World War II the owners of the old Greene Line Steamers, whose overnight passenger steamboats had sometime earlier left the rivers, learned that the *Delta Queen* was for sale. Built more than 75 years ago as a car ferry for the Sacramento River in California, conveying vehicles and passengers to San Francisco, she had then been put into service with the United States Navy during the war, wearing battleship gray under her conversion.

The Greenes bought her and had her towed down the Pacific and through the Panama Canal, then brought up the Mississippi for refitting into an overnight passenger paddlewheeler, her one-time car deck turned into the Orleans Room for dining and entertainment. Over the ensuing years, and through several changes of ownership, she became a familiar sight on the great river and its tributaries. Special acts of Congress gave her protection from Coast Guard regulations that otherwise would have prohibited her largely wooden super-structure, and in 1989 Congress again came to her aid with permanent protection by designating her a National Historic Landmark.

Meanwhile her owners had built and put into operation a much larger sister ship, the *Mississippi Queen*, and then in 1995 they launched the even grander *American Queen*, the largest passenger steamboat ever to ply the rivers. Together, the three beautiful ladies, all driven by steam, have opened up a new world of travel and culture for their passengers, for whom steamboating now is not transportation from one port to another, but a journey from our own time into the past. Each boasts a fine menu, a variety of on-board entertainment, and year-round access to the heartland of America. Indeed, every now and then one of the boats has opened up a "new" river, one not traveled before, and the excitement among regular steamboaters is palpable.

Occasionally, as here, all three of the *Queens* steam together for the camera, or tie up together in port, a memorable event not just for their passengers but for the people on shore who always flock to the banks whenever one of the *Queens* passes. As long as these boats still churn the brown waters of the rivers, and as long as Americans continue their fascination with them, then steamboating will never die.

TOURING ON THE
AMERICAN QUEEN

Overnight passenger steamboats all but disappeared from the rivers before World War II, though some barge tow boats continued to provide a few cabins for travelers. Railroads and later aircraft simply took over American transportation. By the 1960s there was only one left, the old *Delta Queen*, a ferry converted to carry over 100 passengers on "steamboatin'" tours on the Mississippi and Ohio, and tributaries. Old and expensive to operate, she was designated a National Historic Landmark in 1989. In 1974 her owners launched a new and much more modern sternwheeler, the *Mississippi Queen*, capable of carrying nearly 400 passengers, and dramatically expanding river touring by steamboat for those who could afford the excursions.

Then in 1995 they launched the *American Queen*, built in Louisiana and headquartered in New Orleans. She is a floating palace, with a theater, gentlemen's and ladies' salons, a library, a lavish dining room, a galleried show room, exercise room, swimming pool, and accommodations for more than 400 passengers in state rooms reminiscent of the rivers and river towns of America. The history of steamboating is commemorated throughout, from the dining room named for Captain John W. Cannon's grand *J. M. White*, to the cases of museum exhibits in the Mark Twain Gallery. State rooms are decorated with antiques and reproductions reminiscent of the Victorian era heyday of the riverboats, and a resident "riverlorian" interprets the story of the rivers, past and present, for the passengers.

The *American Queen* plies the rivers from New Orleans to St. Paul, from Pittsburgh to Cairo, and has even ventured up the Tennessee River to Chattanooga. Passengers are entertained by nightly shows in the Grand Saloon, visiting lectures and musical events, as well as shore tours at ports along the way from battlefields at Vicksburg and Port Hudson to the fine mansions of Natchez and St. Francisville. It is a long way from the steamboating experiences of past generations of Americans, but still the flavor and lure of the rivers remain alive, reflected in the mist that hovers above the *American Queen*'s paddlewheel, the latest, but surely not the last, of the thousands that have churned the rivers for nearly two centuries.

INDEX

180

PICTURE CREDITS

The publishers wish to thank the following individuals and collections for supplying and permitting the use of illustrations used in this book, as follows:

The Delta Quen Riverboat Company: pages 138-139, 140-141.

Collection of Thomas H. Gandy and Joan W. Gandy: pages 78-79, 86-87, 91, 102-103, 110-111 (top), 118-119, 122-123.

The Missouri Historical Society: page 77 (bottom).

Murphy Library, University of Wisconsin - La Crosse: pages 22-23, 28-29, 35 (bottom), 36-37, 81, 128-129.

The Naval Photographic Center, Department of the Navy: page 15 (center).

Public Library of Cincinnati and Hamilton County: pages 24-25.

U.S. Army Military History Institute: pages 40-41, 56-57.

The U.S. Library of Congress: pages 1, 4, 6, 8, 9, 10, 11, 12, 13. 14-15 (bottom), 15 top, 16, 17, 19 (bottom), 20-21 (bottom), 21 (top right), 33, 35 (top), 39, 58-59, 62-63, 64-=65, 66-67, 68-69, 71, 72-73, 76-77 (top), 82-83, 84-85, 88-89, 94-95, 99, 100-101, 104-105, 106-107, 108-109, 111 (bottom), 112-113, 116-117, 121 (bottom), 124-125, 132-133, 134-135.

The U.S. National Archives: pages 1, 3, 18 (top), 21 (top left), 42-43, 44-45, 46-47, 48-49, 50-51, 52-53, 54-55, 60-61, 96-97.

Winona County Historical Society: pages 30-31, 75, 92-93, 114-115, 120-121 (top), 127, 130-131.

J. Miles Wolf: pages 136-137.